ROAD TO FREEDOM

The Origins of Australia's Most Successful Political Party

J. R. Nethercote

Nick Cater

Published by Connor Court Publishing under the imprint: Jeparit Press 2019

Jeparit Press is an imprint of Connor Court Publishing in association with the Menzies Research Centre

CONNOR COURT PUBLISHING PTY LTD
PO Box 7257
Redland Bay QLD 4165

sales@connorcourt.com

www.connorcourtpublishing.com.au

ISBN: 9781925826715

Cover design by Vanessa Schimizzi

Printed in Australia

LIBERAL PARTY OF AUSTRALIA

75TH ANNIVERSARY

ROAD TO FREEDOM

The Origins of Australia's Greatest Political Party

J. R. Nethercote

Nick Cater

In this free society, the tyrannical notion of an all-powerful State is rejected and dogmatic socialism with it. In its place, we have put opportunity without any class privilege, social and economic justice, and the civilised democratic conception that governments are not the masters of the people, but their servants.

Robert Menzies, The Liberal Creed, Hotel Canberra, 6 April 1964

CONTENTS

1

Liberalism

The Idea that united a movement and inspired a nation

Nick Cater

In the final months of World War II, in a room above a department store in the country town of Albury, a new political party was born that was to dominate Australian politics for the next three quarters of a century.

Within five years of its formation, the Liberal Party of Australia and the Country Party Coalition was in federal government and would remain there for the next 23 years.

The party's founder and intellectual leader, Sir Robert Menzies, served as prime minister for 16 of those years.

On the eve of the party's 75th anniversary, it can justifiably claim not only to be the natural party of federal government in Australia but the most successful centre-right force in the English-speaking world.

Since World War II the Liberal Party has served in government for longer than any other centre-right party in the Anglosphere. It has won considerably more elections than any other party. Its philosophy of putting the instincts and enterprise of individuals ahead of the organising state has become the default setting for the management of civic affairs.

The Liberal Party's partnership with the Country Party, now the Nationals, has been vital to its success. No other coalition in the democratic world has been so enduring that it demands to be spelt with an upper-case "C". The partnership pre-dates formation of the Liberal Party by more than 20 years and will shortly celebrate its centenary.

The fruits of this union and the permanency of the Liberal ideal have been a level of political stability that is unique in the democratic world. It has laid the foundation for a strong economy by encouraging and rewarding enterprise, eschewing central planning and taxing prudently.

It created the conditions that allowed Australia's middle class to become the most prosperous in the world, with wealth spread more evenly than in most comparable economies. It is a country where effort is rewarded but the welfare of all is protected.

The party's work is far from completed. It enters the final quarter of its first century with a strong mandate to create further opportunity by fostering an atmosphere in which individuals and businesses can thrive. Its founding principles have lost none of their potency.

As the Liberal Party celebrates an important anniversary it can justifiably take pride in having fulfilled Menzies' promise: to make Australia more prosperous and just.

Origins

The modest, unimposing setting for the Liberal Party's first conference in December 1944 reflected the founding values and the character of its first leader.

"I do not believe that the real life of this nation is to be found either in great luxury hotels and the petty gossip of so-called fashionable suburbs," Menzies had said in 1942. True to that principle, the fledging party hired a wood-panelled, first-floor lounge above the Mates Emporium on the corner of Dean and Keiwa streets in Albury for the events. It had been advertised for hire in the local newspaper for "receptions, bridge parties, or meetings of croquet, hockey or tennis clubs."

When the building was opened 13 years earlier it contained at least one luxury feature, the town's first electric lift, praised in a local newspaper for its "entire absence of vibration on a trip that seemed all too short."

It was in this unpretentious location in a town with a population of 10,000 people that representatives from 18 different non-Labor organisations arrived on December 14, 1944, many of them on a train aptly called the Spirit of Progress.

Most of the groundwork towards creating the party had already been completed by the time delegates had arrived in Albury. The choice of the name "Liberal", in preference to

Conservative, had already been made. Menzies' explanation for that is contained in a chapter in his book *Afternoon Light*, which is reproduced in this volume. The Albury conference marked the party's formal foundation with the adoption of a constitution and platform.

They shared a single aim: to form a national political party that would support individual rather than collective interests. "If we stand for anything as Liberals we stand for the inescapable responsibility of the individual, his dignity, his significance, his responsibility to every other individual," Robert Menzies told the closing session, four days before his 50th birthday.

The Morning Border Mail wished them every success in its editorial: "The citizens of this town hope to be able to say: 'This is where political history was made'."

The enduring Liberal idea

Three-quarters of a century after the Liberal Party's birth, it is time for a reassessment of its fortunes. Too much of the history of this period has been written from a progressive perspective in which the electoral success of the Liberal Party is due solely to the Labor Party's failure. It became a common explanation for the Liberal Party's first election victory in 1949 and was thriving again 70 years later after Prime Minister Scott Morrison's victory in an election most commentators expected him not to win.

John Nethercote's account of the 1949 election paints the Liberal Party's success in a more convincing light. Labor's overreach, notably with its plan to nationalise the banks, was indeed a factor in Menzies' success. The party's appeal ran far deeper than that, however. Menzies' opposition to socialism and the welfare state resonated in a country with a large middle class, either migrants themselves or the sons and daughters of migrants, blessed with the spirit of pioneers.

Menzies had conducted a clever campaign, sophisticated for its day and relatively well funded. Yet he did not spin his way to power; he won the Australian people over through argument and persuasion. He constructed a solid intellectual base for the party through a series of popular radio broadcasts on the Macquarie Radio Network, the most famous of which was the Forgotten People broadcast of May 22, 1942. Menzies' interpretation of liberalism – regarding freedom of speech, religion, and association, the freedom of citizens to choose their own way of life and the encouragement of individual enterprise as the motive power of economic progress – was consistently articulated at a popular level for more than seven years before the party's electoral success.

They were not novel ideas. Their intellectual antecedence can be traced back to classical liberalism that flourished in the 17th century during the period known as the Enlightenment.

The ideas in which Menzies anchored the party and the history of their arrival and development in Australia are explored by David Kemp in his five-volume history of Australian liberalism. The central values are the worth and dignity of every individual and the equal rights of all to control their own lives. The principle that individuals must be protected from the exercise of arbitrary powers by others, notably by the state, is intrinsic to liberalism.

Menzies applied this philosophy to the circumstances of his time. It was the central core around which the disparate parties of the centre-right were able to unite in 1944 in the newly formed Liberal Party of Australia. They were the principles that appealed to the Australian people in 1949, motivated by the universal desire of humans to control their own lives.

At a time when the international trend in democracy was towards granting greater powers to the state, the newly formed Liberal Party offered a different path. It rejected the centrally planned economy as unworkable. Policy that punished thrift and encouraged dependence on the state in pursuit of "dull equality" was "the quintessence of madness," said Menzies. Instead, the Liberal Party sought to empower an ambitious middle class, "frugal people who strive for and obtain the margin above these materially necessary things," as the foundation for an active and developing national life.

A prosperous Australia

Under the policies embraced by the Coalition and on occasions by Labor since 1949, Australia has achieved an exceptional growth in prosperity that marks it apart from much of the developed world. Recessions in general have been shorter, less frequent and less severe than in Europe and the United States. Periods of growth have been longer. Australians have been blessed for most of the postwar years by full employment.

The prosperity that flows from this has spread widely; wealth is commoner in the Commonwealth of Australia than the Labor Party wants you to think.

Two-thirds of Australian adults (67 per cent) have a net worth of more than $100,000, a higher percentage than in any other country. By comparison, Canada has only 51 per cent, New Zealand 50, the US 41 and Sweden 35.

Australia is third highest on the list of 41 industrialised countries when it comes to the even distribution of wealth measured by the Gini coefficient. Sweden, the social justice poster nation of the Left, is fourth from bottom, ignobly between India and Turkey.

Australia ties with the US in second place on the ladder measuring proportion of population worth more than $US1 million. Most of that money is invested in residential real estate.

Australia's super-rich, frequently demonised as the so-called one per cent, are the fifth poorest in the industrialised world. They account for 22 per cent of the nation's wealth. In Russia, which spent seven fruitless decades in a nominal journey towards equality under communism, the one percenters own 57 per cent of the wealth. In the social democratic paradise of Sweden they own 37 percent.

The triumph of the Australian middle class is a vindication of Liberal policies and defiance of socialism. It has been achieved in an atmosphere where private entrepreneurialism has been allowed to thrive. Risk is rewarded and private savings recognised. Our current wealth is built not on luck or cronyism but on the savings of the past.

The middle class, Menzies said, was envied "by those whose benefits are largely obtained by taxing them." At the 2019 election, the Liberal Party rejected Labor's so-called "fair-go economics" as fraudulent. It was presented as an exercise in redistributing money from rich to poor but its effect would have been very different. It would have expanded and emboldened the public sector at the expense of a dispirited middle class.

A just Australia

Prudent government spending is an enduring feature of Liberal governments, albeit with some breaches. It stems less from a dogmatic belief in small government than from a conviction that a government must be a responsible steward of public funds. "Governments, contrary to a well-known political superstition, have no money of their own," Menzies said. "They spend what men and women have earned and have paid to them in either taxes or loans."[1]

The Liberal Party's role in government amounts to far more than balancing the books, however. Its founding proposition was not economic in character, but moral. For Menzies, the responsibility of a Liberal government was to advance social as well as economic justice. The party's founders were not insensitive to the plight of those who, for any reason, struggle to overcome the friction of everyday life. They rejected the unrealisable and ultimately undesirable idea that all should be rewarded equally. Instead they built a moral case for egalitarianism, a conviction stemming from the New Testament that every individual was equal before God. Transposed for a secular democracy, this philosophy demands that we strive for social equality, instating that every human being be endowed with equal opportunity, limited only by the capacity of our imperfect civic institutions to live up to this high ideal.

It has been fashionable in recent years to belittle the achievements of the Liberal Party in its first 40 years because

---

1 Robert Menzies, 'The Science and Art of Politics', University of Texas Lectures (No 1), 20 November 1969

of its alleged failure to conform to modern economic doctrine. The criticisms frequently rely on a sub-prime understanding of both the economic achievements of the Menzies years and the economics of the Chicago School that informed the deregulatory reforms of the 1980s and 1990s. The most significant confusion, however, is the assumption that our present prosperity stems from a doctrinaire commitment to market freedom and a rejection of any moves by the state that constrain the right of business to run its own race. This confusion hardened in the 1980s, when the Liberal Party was divided between economic wets and dries, importing the language adopted by the British Conservative Party at the time of Margaret Thatcher.

Today's policy challenges demand a reappraisal of the meaning of economic freedom and the reasons for the Liberal Party's evident success in winning elections and driving prosperity for the past 70 years.

It calls for us to reconsider the duty of Liberal governments to protect citizens from tyranny, the imposition of arbitrary power by institutions. In 1949, the threat of arbitrary power came chiefly from a Labor government, encouraged by a false belief that the wisdom of the state was greater than the collective wisdom of its citizens. Among the hottest political issues of the day was Labor's policy of nationalising the banks. The Liberal Party was implacably opposed by this adventurous public-sector assault on the private sector, which would have stripped competition from the banking market to the detriment of the economy and citizens.

At the 2019 election, the landscape of power was different. The threat of arbitrary power by the state posed by an interventionist Labor platform had not diminished. Yet there was also a threat from the private sector to the freedom of citizens from the arbitrary powers large corporations have assumed in imperfect markets. The debate about the conduct of the banks and energy companies stemmed from the need to protect the interests of consumers against unnaturally powerful corporations in uncompetitive markets.

The freedom of individuals is also under threat from trade unions, which would have become more powerful under a Labor government. Today's trade unions have grown into quasi-corporations riddled with vested interests that, left unchecked, can run roughshod over the rights of others, including their own members.

The rise of cashed-up professional activist groups presents another threat to the civic order. It was vividly on display during the election where activists used dubious tactics to try to sway voters. It is present too in the legal and corporate activism that threatens to stop legitimate investment in the resources sector approved by a democratically elected government.

The threat of arbitrary power is implicit in the rise of so-called political correctness and identity politics. The identity and the motives of the institutions that are driving this are frequently unclear. Many Australians, however, feel acutely that decisions over social mores and education are being made by other people.

It is against this background that Scott Morrison's victory must be assessed. The political and cultural agenda is far more diverse than it was in 1949. In part that has been enabled by social media, the decreasing homogeneity of our society, a general neglect of the national interest and the favouring of special interests.

In the end, however, the Liberal Party won by standing up for the same people Menzies called upon 70 years earlier; the Forgotten People now renamed as the Quiet Australians.

By remaining faithful to the forgotten middle class, the Liberal Party has won 19 out of 29 federal elections since 1946. If this term of government runs its full course, the Coalition will have been in power for twice as long as Labor by the time of the next election.

This an achievement to be celebrated without recourse to hubris. The Liberal Party is successful when it stays true to the voters to whom it owes its success, "the great and sober and dynamic middle-class," as Menzies described. "We shall destroy them," he warned, "at our peril.

2

1949
No Ordinary Swing of the Pendulum

J. R. Nethercote

Prologue

Australia went to the polls on Saturday 10 December 1949. A regular triennial election, the incumbent Labor Government led by Ben Chifley, Prime Minister since 1945, was seeking a third consecutive victory.

Its opponent was a coalition of the Liberal and Country parties led by Robert Menzies, previously prime minister, 1939-41. He had been Leader of the Opposition since 1943. His party, the Liberal Party of Australia, which had replaced the United Australia Party (UAP), was contesting only its second election since formation in 1944-45.

When Menzies opened the Coalition campaign a month out from polling day, he cast the contest starkly:

> Are we for the Socialist State, with its subordination of the individual to the universal officialdom of government, or are we for the ancient British faith that

governments are the servants of the people . . .?[1]

The result answered his question without any equivocation. It was a convincing victory for the Coalition. It secured a majority of 26 in a House of Representatives recently enlarged from 75 to 121 members (and two members from the A. C. T. and the Northern Territory with limited voting rights). As a consequence of staggered terms and a new method of electing senators, the new Government lacked a majority in the Senate where it was outnumbered 34 to 26 notwithstanding having won majorities in five of the six States.

In the years following the Second World War the Labor Government had adopted collectivist policies marked by increasing government intervention in the economy, additional powers for the Commonwealth in the Federation, programs of enhanced government ownership, most notably its attempt to nationalise the private banks, and a preference in international relations for acting within and through the newly-created United Nations. Its record domestically was contentious, notably for continuation of war-time controls (particularly petrol rationing) and industrial unrest, so disruptive in mining that it had been necessary to bring in the Army.

The Liberal challenge to Labor, exemplified by Menzies' radio talks, *The Forgotten People*, was founded upon faith in individual enterprise, endeavour, opportunity and choice.[2]

It was about "encouragement by all possible means of thrift, independence and the family home."

Internationally the Liberals were particularly anxious about the threat of communism, both the tensions in Eastern

Europe and the communist takeover of China in October 1949.

Australia's emerging role in Asia figured prominently; as it happened, one of the first initiatives of the Coalition once back in government was the Columbo Plan, a major foreign aid scheme.

The 1949 election had presented the voters of Australia with an especially clear choice between collectivist policies on the one hand and, on the other, philosophies based on individualism and private enterprise. The Liberal victory was in the vanguard of stemming collectivism in the post-war years.

The result was, thereby, more than a periodical swing of the electoral pendulum in Australia. Labor ruled in three States, Queensland, New South Wales and Tasmania. It had lost office in Western Australia in April 1947 and in Victoria late in 1947; the new Party's hold on power in each was tenuous, however. While the Liberal Country League was entrenched in South Australia, its electoral support was, in fact, weak.

Internationally, collectivist policies still prevailed. In Britain, the Conservatives, out of office since 1945, did not regain office until 1951 (after yet another defeat in 1950); but their policies, economic and social, were in many respects a continuation of those of the Labour Government. The Conservative disposition of the period might most usefully be characterised as "Tory paternalism."

The centre-left Liberal Party of Canada, in office since 1935, won elections in 1949 and 1953. There was no revival of its opponent, the Progressive Conservatives, either philosophically or organisationally, comparable to that wrought by Menzies as he built the Liberal Party upon the wreckage of its predecessor, the United Australia Party. It was only a combination of complacency and exhaustion that brought them back to government unexpectedly in 1957.

In the United States, Republican bids to contain the Democratic ascendancy which began with Roosevelt's New Deal increasingly put their faith in a candidate of proven national stature, in the event, the war hero, General Dwight D. Eisenhower.

Ten days before Australians voted in 1949 New Zealanders went to the polls. The Labour Party, which had first won office in 1935, was defeated. Its vote fell by more than four percent and its seats in the NZ House of Representatives dropped from 42 to 34. The National Party, with a 4.5 percent increase in its vote, now had eight more seats (from 38 to 46), a majority of 12 in the House.

This result had some affinity with the contest in Australia, particularly in the slow lifting of war-time controls. But there had been nothing to compare with bank nationalisation and the Labour Government, worried by the international situation, even proposed introducing conscription. Nationalist rhetoric echoed that of its Australian counterparts: the leader, Sidney Holland, told an audience in 1948, "If you want to condense our policy, it is the private ownership of production, distribution and exchange."

But, as one historian commented, he was "pragmatic . . . Other policies verged on being bipartisan, at least to the level of party leadership, related to defence and foreign affairs." (It is of interest that one of the first actions of the new Nationalist government was to abolish the Legislative Council, an appointed upper chamber: historian Michael

King has commented, "this was a surprising move to come from a conservative government. . . ."[3]

If the collectivist tide had started to ebb, it was with the 1949 result in Australia that this was most evident. It was a result which signalled the renaissance of Liberalism, philosophically, and in advocacy and campaigning. And it brought a completely fresh approach to party organisation grounded in membership, branches and financial independence; it was an approach fully attuned to democratic parliamentary governance.

This Liberal Party, founded upon this trilogy of philosophy, advocacy and organisation, was the singular achievement of Menzies and took its place in the national politics of Australia at a critical time in the battles over collectivism and individualism.

It is the purpose of this essay to tell the story of the course of politics in Australia which culminated in the triumph of the Liberal Party, in coalition with the Country Party, on 10 December 1949.

Election day, 10 December 1949: *one of the great decisive political battles*

On Saturday 10 December 1949, Australians had been to the polls to vote for a new Commonwealth Parliament.

It was a polling day not without its hurdles for the voters. It was the first election since the House of Representatives had been expanded from 75 seats to more than 120; perhaps as many as half the electors were voting in a seat different to that of 1946, the previous general election.

The Senate had likewise been increased, from 36 to 60. Moreover, there was a new method of voting for Senators and, combining proportional and preferential systems (technically known as the single transferable vote), it was more complicated; some voters, especially the elderly, were confused.

Late in the evening reporters gathered outside the Liberal Party's Women's Auxiliary Room at Howey Court in Collins Street, Melbourne. They wanted a statement from Robert Menzies, the Leader of the Opposition and leader of the Liberal Party since its foundation in 1944-45. It seemed, as counting proceeded, that Menzies was destined for a big victory and a return to the prime ministership which he had previously held from April 1939 until August 1941.

Menzies' jubilation was tempered by exhaustion. Barely had the campaign started than he was forced to take nearly a week's rest owing to a bout of flu. But thereafter Menzies campaigned relentlessly, often travelling several hundred miles a day, and addressing as many as five or even six meetings.

On polling day he had voted in the morning at the Congregational Church hall on Burke Street, Deepdene, in his electorate of Kooyong. His daughter, Heather, casting a ballot for the first time, had accompanied him to the polling station. In the evening she had remained at the new family home, Clovelly, in Balwyn, to which the Menzies had moved in September, "looking after," as the *Age* put it, "the crowds of friends and relatives who'd dropped in!"

Menzies' Herculean labours of the previous six years since he became Leader of the Opposition were about to reap their reward. The Opposition, a coalition of the Liberal Party and the Country Party, was poised for victory; in the event the new Coalition Government won with a majority of 26 in the new House of 123 seats. The Labor Government, led by Prime Minister and Treasurer Ben Chifley, was comprehensively defeated.

Menzies eventually broke his silence. He spoke briefly:

> It looks like a great victory.
>
> I adhere to my view that this election was one of the great decisive political battles.
>
> My colleagues and I will take up our great task with a deep sense of responsibility but also a feeling of thankfulness for the deliverance of Australia from the growth of the all-powerful State.

Indeed, the result on 10 December 1949 was not an ordinary victory, especially not for Menzies. He still had "acute memories"[4] of his first precarious prime ministership, a disappointing experience and eventually one of despair. Moreover, this was the third time that he had led the coalition forces in a general election. But, while he had had victories in various referendums of the Curtin and Chifley Labor governments seeking to alter the Australian Constitution, this was the first time he had a clear and indisputable win in an election. And it was conclusive.

This victory was a triumph of purposeful, strategic leadership over more than half a decade. The achievement was manifest in terms of philosophy and advocacy, and of party organisation, creativity and campaigning. During these years Menzies re-established his standing in the country, recovered the leadership of his party, and then recreated it on democratic foundations. The election of 1949 restored him to the prime ministership and a decisive pre-eminence in the national politics of Australia.

Menzies in politics: Victoria

Robert Menzies had entered the House of Representatives a decade and a half earlier, at a general election held in September 1934. He was appointed Attorney-General and Minister for Industry in the re-elected United Australia Party (UAP) Government led by Joseph Lyons. By this time he was already an experienced parliamentarian and minister. First elected to the Legislative Council of Victoria in 1928, he successfully contested a seat in the Legislative Assembly the following year and spent a term in opposition.

During these years he embarked on his first exercise in party-building, the Young Nationalists. This endeavour was so successful that when, in 1932, the party under Stanley Argyle won office, Menzies was able to claim not only the attorney-generalship but also the deputy premiership.

And it was not only at State level that Menzies was active. From late 1930 and throughout 1931, the Scullin Labor Government, which had come to office federally in October 1929, increasingly fell into disarray. Menzies was the leading figure in a group otherwise composed of businessmen who exploited the prospects of splitting federal Labor and forcing an election.

Two senior ministers, Joseph Lyons and James Fenton, resigned from the Government on 4 February 1931. Respectively Postmaster-General and Minister for Trade and Customs, they had, during Prime Minister Scullin's absence in London at an Imperial Conference, acted as Treasurer and

Prime Minister. A month later they, and three other Labor members, supported an Opposition vote of no confidence.

On 5 May, the Nationalist Party under John Latham merged with the Lyons group as the United Australia Movement, with Lyons as the leader. Following defeat of the Government in a confidence vote on 25 November, an election was called for 19 December 1931. The new United Australia Party (UAP) won office with good majorities in both the House of Representatives and the Senate.

The United Australia Party, like its predecessor, the Nationalist Party, was essentially a parliamentary organisation. A crucial but not its sole weakness was that it had only a most rudimentary branch structure in electorates. A weak organisation, especially in terms of public participation, it was ill-suited to the political life of a parliamentary democracy.

John Howard, a person with deep knowledge and experience of both the organisational and parliamentary sides of politics, captured the failings of the UAP with great cogency:

> It lacked philosophical coherence or any semblance of a national organisation, and had no independent fundraising capacity, thus leaving it particularly vulnerable to pressure groups. . . . it had been created solely to unite Joe Lyons and some of his former Labor colleagues, with the then Nationalist Party. . . once Lyons had gone, its artificial character became apparent. In [Hasluck's] telling phrase, . . . the UAP had been the "progeny of expediency."[5]

Menzies goes to Canberra, 1934

At the next federal election, on 15 September 1934, Menzies replaced former Nationalist leader, John Latham, as the member for Kooyong. Third in order of precedence after the Prime Minister and the Country Party leader, Earle (Sir Earle from 1937) Page, he was appointed Attorney-General and Minister for Industry. A year later he defeated Sir Archdale Parkhill, the leading minister from New South Wales, for the deputy leadership of the parliamentary party.

His rise was not only "very rapid"[6] but immediately took on an international character which largely marked his entire time in the national parliament. In the life of the parliament, 1934-37, he twice travelled to the United Kingdom. His gifts in oratory won him much acclaim in London during the visit in 1935 for celebrations marking the jubilee of His Majesty King George V. His return journey to Australia took him to the United States where he met President Franklin D. Roosevelt at the White House, the first of five Presidents who received him there. He also went to Canada.

On a 1938 visit to Europe, he was not only involved in complex trade negotiations but he visited Nazi Germany at a time when questions concerning eastern Europe were intensifying.

The Coalition Government was, however, increasingly unsettled. Publicly dispute centred upon the proposed National Insurance Scheme whose introduction had been a feature of the UAP campaign at the 1937 election and to which the Country Party was opposed. Other matters in contention concerned the tariff and defence preparations.

Throughout the early months of 1939 Menzies' prospective

departure from the Government was widely reported in newspapers but it was not until 20 March 1939 that he resigned.

1939: Menzies, Prime Minister

Lyons died on Good Friday, 7 April 1939. On 18 April the UAP met. Menzies won the leadership by one vote from the aged veteran, William Morris Hughes, after proposals to recall S. M. Bruce to the leadership did not arouse much support and two Victorians, R. G. Casey, the Treasurer, and T. W. White, a son-in-law of Alfred Deakin, had been eliminated in the early rounds of the ballot which then ensued.[7]

Page, prime minister pending election of a new leader of the UAP, launched a notoriously nasty attack on Menzies. It was disowned not only by the UAP but by two members of the Country Party, one of them Arthur Fadden. As Menzies later commented, Page "did himself more harm than he did me."[8]

Menzies formed his first government, supported by 28 UAP members; "conducting a minority government," he later wrote, "is a great training ground in political tactics."[9] The Country Party, with 14 members, went to the cross-bench; Labor, the Opposition, led by John Curtin from Western Australia had 29 seats but divisions between the federal party and those supporting the former Premier of New South Wales, Jack Lang, had not yet been conclusively resolved.

Menzies, as well as being Prime Minister, was also Treasurer and, after its creation, took the new portfolio of Defence Co-ordination; "it was a strenuous period for me."[10] Major figures in the new ministry included Casey (Supply and Development) until he went to a diplomatic post in

Washington; Geoffrey Street, Minister for the Army; Sir Henry Gullett, External Affairs; and James Fairbairn, Civil Aviation and, later, also Air.

Menzies: his first coalition government, 1940-41

Page, and his deputy Paterson, survived until September 1939 when they were replaced as Country Party leaders by A. G. Cameron and Harold Thorby. On 14 March 1940 a new Coalition Government was established. In an important move in coalition management, Menzies, while agreeing to consult on the personnel of the ministry, made the final decisions himself. (In one other respect, the coalition arrangements included an important qualification on Cabinet responsibility. This was an understanding that Country Party ministers would not be bound to support government legislation for establishment of a motor car industry to which they had already expressed opposition; two months later they voted against the legislation.)

The new ministry had better prospects than its immediate predecessors. With the exception of Hughes, difficult members, in particular, Page, were not included. And there were new ministers who brought youth and vigour, Percy Spender (NSW), as Treasurer, and John McEwen (Vic) as Minister for External Affairs, as well as Arthur Fadden (Qld) and Senator Philip McBride (SA) in junior posts.

Menzies: deserted by fortune

An election was looming but death was stalking the Menzies Government.

Tuesday 13 August 1940 was a bright and sunny day in Canberra and Menzies was at work in his office in Parliament House. Though the Government was in minority, Menzies "had many good friends and colleagues . . . [and several were] men of character, capable of being difficult, but never capable of disloyalty."

> A knock came on my door, and somebody walked in. There had been a dreadful air crash, almost within sight of my windows. Gullett was dead; Street was dead; Fairbairn was dead; . . . Sir Brudenell White, whom I had recalled from retirement to be Chief of the General Staff, was dead. And dead with them were other young men whom I knew, and for whom I had an affection.
>
> This was a dreadful calamity, for my three colleagues were my close and loyal friends; each of them had a place not only in my Cabinet, but in my heart. I shall never forget that terrible hour; I felt that, for me, the end of the world had come . . . In the whole history of government in Australia, this was the most devastating tragedy.[11]

Within a fortnight the House of Representatives was dissolved (27 August 1940) and the country was heading for elections on 21 September. The result was an evenly divided House, Government and Opposition each emerging with 36 seats. There were two independents; one, Arthur Coles, subsequently joined the UAP party room; the other, Wilson, who described himself as an Independent Country Party man, usually voted with the Government. Moreover, Labor had still not yet attained the level of unity which would eventually sustain it in office.

Early the following year Menzies decided to go to London for discussions about defence arrangements in the Far East as well as utilisation of Australian forces in the Middle East and the Mediterranean. He travelled via Singapore, the centrepiece of Imperial defence in the Far East; and the Middle East, where most Australian forces were deployed.

The journey's results were ambiguous. Concerns about defence in the Far East, and particularly the adequacy of Singapore, were confirmed rather than assuaged. Churchill's assurances did not reassure Menzies. He travelled home through the United States, Canada and New Zealand.

The trip has been much criticised and Pattie Menzies' counsel before he went, "If you feel you must go, you will go. But you will be out of office within six weeks of your return," is oft-quoted.[12] The main misjudgement was, however, not necessarily the decision to go, but that he stayed away for too long, particularly after it became clear that Britain, embattled in Europe, the North Atlantic, the Mediterranean, the Middle East and potentially in the Far East, was poorly placed to address Australia's security concerns which were undoubtedly serious but nevertheless, at that stage, not desperately imminent.

Upon return Menzies made major changes to the machinery of government, essentially placing it fully on a war footing. This took the form, in particular, of creation of new departments: Aircraft Production; External Territories; Home Security; Transport; and War Organization of Industry.

The political situation was dire. Menzies' various efforts to establish a national government had been rebuffed and Labor, having largely settled its internal divisions, was more strongly placed to challenge the Government, restrained mainly by John Curtin's reticence.

Both the *Sydney Morning Herald* and papers controlled by Keith Murdoch were increasingly critical. Their criticisms were reflected in the attitudes of the business communities in both Sydney and Melbourne which were percolating into the parliamentary ranks and were readily supported by various members disappointed not to have been included in the ministry when it had been reconstructed in June. Menzies' own mood may be gleaned from a letter to a confidant on 24 July 1941:

> They are ill days for any country when the royal road to publicity, and even, fame, is through disloyalty to your Government, your party and your leader.[13]

Early in August Menzies began an Australia-wide tour to "talk about the war." Japanese advances in Indo-China, and threats to Thailand, led to its early cancellation and Cabinet meetings at which Menzies pressed the question of a return to London because, as he wrote to High Commissioner Bruce, "I am more effective in London than here where at present a hail-fellow-well-met technique is preferred to information or reason."[14]

In the evenly divided House of Representatives Labor's acquiescence was necessary and it was not forthcoming. As a consequence of ensuing Cabinet discussions, including further thought about a national government, Menzies decided to resign in favour of whomever the government parties chose to succeed him (as prime minister; he remained leader of the UAP): " . . . I do believe that my relinquishing of the leadership will offer a real prospect of unity in the ranks of the Government parties. Under these circumstances, and having regard to the grave emergencies of war, my own feelings must be set aside," as he said in a press statement.[15]

Menzies, still leader of the United Australia Party, continued as Minister for Defence Co-ordination until the fall of the Fadden Government and the move into opposition.

Menzies, 1941

As Menzies himself wrote, his fall from office in 1941 "enabled quite a few people to write my political obituary." This had, he continued, "a special effect on a man of contentious capacity and healthy ambition."[16]

There were, nonetheless, several early signs that he was not yet done with parliamentary service. The first followed immediately upon loss of office. Prior to a meeting of the parliamentary UAP he resigned as leader. He immediately, however, urged the party to claim the Leadership of the Opposition as was its prerogative as the most numerous party not in or supporting the incumbent ministry. Menzies recounted the party's reaction:

> My party, by a majority, took the view that as Fadden, leader of the Country Party, had just been Prime Minister, he should become Leader of the Opposition. In what, I suppose, could have been regarded as a high-handed manner (but it must be remembered that, after my still recent experiences, I was in a very exacerbated state of mind), I said, "Well, a party of our numbers which is not prepared to lead is not worth leading."[17]

In the ballot for a new leader, the aged Hughes, on the cusp of his 80th birthday, was elected unanimously. This effectively created a vacuum and politics, like nature, abhors a vacuum. There were few at this time who thought that it would be Menzies himself who would fill the vacuum; those who did so would not have expected him to do so as quickly as he did.

Until the next election, Menzies "sat in a back seat on the Opposition side of the House as a private member."[18]

Two important other signs that Menzies, at the very most, was highly ambivalent about leaving politics in Australia concerned prospective appointments abroad, the first, a British interest in appointing him as UK Minister of State in South-East Asia; the second was appointment as Australian Minister in Washington, replacing Casey who had taken a post as UK Minister of State in the Middle East.

To the first proposition, Menzies responded that as "[he] had shot [his] bolt in his own country [he] would be more than happy to serve some useful purpose somewhere." But nothing eventuated before the fall of Singapore in February 1942 and Japanese occupation of New Guinea; he remained in the House of Representatives.[19]

To the Washington suggestion, he informed Curtin that if "[he] were offered the American post, [he] would give the offer the fullest consideration."[20] There was never any offer.

A further indication of his continuing commitment to Australian political life came when he agreed to continue as a member of the Advisory War Council, a Government-Opposition consultative body established after the 1940 election when Labor refused to join a national government.

At the end of October 1941, within a month of losing office,

Menzies spoke in the House on the revised Budget which Chifley had introduced. In the next two years Menzies, as his principal biographer, A. W. Martin, noted, "lapsed into comparative silence."[21] Yet the speech on the Budget showed the seeds of what was to come. The tax burden as proposed by Chifley, would bear heavily on families and on those who lacked the protection of unions:

> Every one of us, whether it be the man who lives in Bellevue Hill on an income of 15 000 pounds, or the girl who earns three pounds a week as a stenographer, must be prepared to say "I have a contribution to make."
>
> I am not afraid to go out and say that to the people of Australia.[22]

The Forgotten People

Silent he may have been in the Parliament but early in 1942 he took to the airwaves in a series of short weekly broadcasts now known as *The Forgotten People* (the seminal address which gave its name to a book in which a very broad selection is published). His central theme was simply and clearly stated:

> I do not believe that the real life of this nation is to be found either in great luxury hotels and the petty gossip of so-called fashionable suburbs, or in the officialdom of organized masses. It is to be found in the homes of people who are nameless and unadvertised, and who, whatever their religious conviction or dogma, see in their children their greatest contribution to the immortality of their race. The home is the foundation of sanity and sobriety; it is the indispensable condition of continuity; its health determines the health of society as a whole.[23]

He later distilled the essence of freedom, which had become an underlying theme in his oratory:

> There may be some people who think the only freedom that counts is to have a roof to sleep under, clothes to wear, food to eat. These are very necessary. Governments must be pledged to do all in their power to assist people to secure them; but they are not freedoms at all. Each can be obtained in a state of utter slavery.
>
> The real freedoms are to worship, to think, to speak, to choose, to be ambitious, to be independent, to be industrious, to acquire skill, to seek reward. These are the real freedoms, for these are the essence of the nature of man.[24]

In these speeches Menzies had identified the broad citizenry to whom he spoke and for whom he spoke, the individual, and the individual and the family. He spoke for talent, for education, for industry, for enterprise, for "a decent and reasonable minimum of economic security and material well-being" and for "an enlightened citizenship based upon honest thinking and human understanding."

The strength of the broadcasts was in taking various matters pertinent to Australian society of the 1930s and 1940s, reflecting upon how they might be addressed, with a simply expressed foundation in principle and philosophy, and an exposition of how "salary-earners, shopkeepers, skilled artisans, professional men and women, farmers, and so on" are affected:

> They are, in the political and economic sense, the middle class. They are for the most part unorganized and unself-conscious. They are envied by those whose social benefits are largely obtained by taxing them.

> They are not rich enough to have individual power.
> They are taken for granted by each political party in
> turn . . . And yet, as I have said, they are the backbone
> of the nation.[25]

As Howard has rightly observed: "His arguments were lucidly put, with just enough policy content to give the listener a clear idea of where Menzies stood, but without so much detail as to leave Menzies hostage to future nit-picking from his opponents."[26]

Allan Martin, seeing the speeches as "a powerful piece of political propaganda," thought it was "Menzies at his best: . . . presenting simple, arresting ideas in elegant, ardent language. It has the ring of sincerity because so much of it is in fact autobiographical."[27]

Martin's view is borne out by other activities.

As early as April 1942 Menzies signalled a continuing interest in party leadership. He told Hughes, the UAP leader, that he was

> . . . not proposing to become a candidate for the
> leadership of the Party, but if at any time in the future
> circumstances arose under which for any reason
> the Party, *as a Party*, requested me to resume the
> leadership, I would feel obliged to do so, provided I
> thought the request represented the real will of the
> party, but not otherwise. [emphasis in original][28]

Hughes, thanking him for his letter, nonetheless noted the "pregnant but ambiguous qualification."

Menzies' thinking about the future was by no means confined to the broadcasts. In July 1942 he drafted "Commonwealth Opposition Policy for 1942-3" and presented it to the Party

Executive (of which he was a member for a time). Generally well-received, one member commented that: "I think it good and trust that it will be adopted without stupid manipulation or additions of supposedly vote catching nostrums. If we attempt to outbid Labor we are licked before we start; it can't be done and anyhow, W. M. H. notwithstanding, most of us, I hope value self respect."[29]

Menzies may have been sitting on the backbench. But he was already leading the party in philosophy and policy. He was laying the foundations for what would become the victory of 10 December 1949.

The paper, adopted in August 1942, was already looking beyond the next election, even beyond the war, to a time when Labor could well be contemplating use of war-time powers long after there was any war to give rise to a need for them. It warned:

> All our short term activity should be conducted against a background of long term policy so that the people may see not only what we are doing but in what direction we are travelling. . . .

> The dynamic section of Labour, under [Eddie]Ward [Minister for Labour and National Service], is plainly out not for old-fashioned democratic socialism, but for a syndicalist system in which industrial and business control will pass into the hands of Trades Unions and Trade Union officials, thrift will be penalised, and the great middle class of people crushed. We should, to counter this plan – which wartime conditions are powerfully assisting – set out certain principles which will inform our own postwar programmes.[30]

Short-term objectives included taxation on a wider field than at present; the outlawing of strikes; resistance to compulsory unionism; research in preparation for post-war reconstruction. Long-term aims included achievement of secret ballots in unions; simpler arbitration machinery; national insurance on a contributory basis; and "the encouragement by all possible means of thrift, independence and the family home."[31]

The National Service Group

It was one proposal in the Opposition policy paper which showed Menzies increasingly resuming the mantle of leadership. The paper advocated a single Australian Army, thus incorporating the militia which included conscripted soldiers who could not be deployed outside Australia.

Curtin, a leading anti-conscriptionist during the Great War, proposed to extend the zone in which conscripts could be deployed to include Timor, Amboina and Dutch New Guinea. The UAP thought that Australian soldiers, volunteer and conscript, should be liable for all areas in which the Japanese had to be fought.

The party majority, however, was reluctant to press for amendments lest Curtin's opponents in the Labor Party exploited the move to have the Government's modest proposals abandoned. Those in the UAP who wanted a stronger stand, including Menzies, Percy Spender and Archie Cameron, initially acquiesced, but soon repented on the basis that "this is a world war, and that no limit can be set in the duty of Australia in relation to it."[32] Hughes bitterly resented the initiative. He was forced to call the first party meeting since he had captured the leadership.

It was a "singularly disagreeable" experience according to

Menzies. His supporters wanted to seek a spill of positions, very unusual at that stage of Australian politics, but Menzies dissuaded them because of the bitter hostility which would be fomented, a sign of a new maturity in his handling of party situations, a consciousness of the folly of striking before the time was ripe. Thus the attempt to unseat Hughes was defeated, ironically, by Menzies' own friends.[33]

It was another mark of Menzies' astuteness that he exploited the situation for positive purpose. On 1 April 1943, with 16 of his colleagues, he published a statement of broad policy, but relating particularly to an enlarged role for Australia internationally, and specifically within a United Nations context; creation of one Australian Army; broader taxation to finance the war; restricted spending on any other government programs until the war was over; and measures to deal with industrial disorder on the minefields and on the wharves.

The signatories called themselves the National Service Group. Among those who supported the statement were Victorian Senators John Spicer and Senator Leckie (Menzies' father-in-law), and Eric Harrison (NSW). 10 of the 17 came from South Australia. Neither Percy Spender nor Harold Holt signed. Fadden held aloof, deeming the matter one for the UAP, but Hughes denounced it as the work of a "Group of Wreckers." Showing that, whatever else, his formidable skills in invective remained in good order, he asserted that the Group would be "as helpless in the House of Representatives as a beetle on its back."[34]

Shortly afterwards Menzies issued a manifesto, again advancing *Forgotten People* themes:

> We must abandon the suicidal policy of wiping out the
> middle class of people. Why should they who have no
> unions, who draw fixed salaries or modest incomes,
> who get no cost of living adjustments . . . be required
> at a time like this to dig into their pockets in order that
> the waterside workers should be paid amazing wages,
> or dissipate their own hard-earned savings so that
> somebody else should get a bigger free pension.[35]

The National Service Group ceased attending either UAP or
joint party meetings. But the political realities were very much
on display when late in June 1943 Fadden moved a formal
no-confidence motion in the House of Representatives; the
second speaker for the Opposition was not Hughes, as might
have been expected, but Menzies.

The 1943 election

The House was dissolved early in July 1943 for an election on
21 August. The Opposition parties were poorly prepared in
terms of either policy or organization. The UAP, Menzies
wrote, "had behind it (more or less) a whole series of
unrelated organizations, without cohesion or common
purpose."[36]

While Hughes hardly campaigned Menzies –

> . . . worked hard: during five weeks of continuous
> campaigning he spoke in five States and travelled over
> 7000 miles. Of the fifty meetings he addressed, . . . "only
> two were badly obstructed." With these exceptions, his
> audiences were "mostly friendly in character. There
> was certainly no superficial sign of any swing in the
> direction of Labour."[37]

It was all to little avail. Labor had a great win, comparable to

Andrew Fisher's victories in 1910 and 1914. With a favourable swing of 7.9 percent (estimated two-party-preferred) the Government won 49 of the 75 seats in the House, up from 36 in the previous parliament. UAP representation fell from 23 to 12; the Country Party retained 12 seats. In the Senate, Labor won all 19 vacancies.

Though the word most frequently used to describe the result was "deluge" – Menzies himself called it a "debacle"[38] - the defeated Opposition leadership was still able to look with satisfaction on its performance. Fadden wrote to Hughes that he was "quite confident that nothing can be laid at our door with regard to the disastrous result of the elections." The fault lay with the National Service Group, particularly on the Militia question. "As long as we stick together I feel we can rebuild something out of the ruins. We shall have to look to the future instead of holding futile post-mortems, out of which no good can come."[39]

Fadden had spoken too soon. Others saw post-mortems as the key. To Menzies, "the wreck produced by the election gives us a great opportunity, if we are ready to seize it," to "establish a new party under a new name," remedying the lack of viable Opposition party organization and ideology.[40]

Menzies: Leader of the Opposition, 1943

Settling the party leadership was the first hurdle to overcome. Hughes was wily to the last. His first gambit was to raise the question of continuing the joint opposition with the Country Party. The possibility of merger also came up. Menzies' report of the meeting gives it a surreal quality:

> I allowed confusion to develop, holding my fire to the

very last moment. Billy, in the Chair, was incredible. His grasp of procedure has never been very great, and the task of determining in what order and how you put to a meeting of reasonably talkative men a motion, an amendment, an amendment on an amendment to the motion proved entirely beyond him. For once I was sensible . . . and did nothing to extract him from the tangle, having a vague idea in my mind that his claims to lead an outnumbered party in the hurly burly of Parliamentary debate were rapidly fading.[41]

Menzies succeeded in having all motions before the meeting thrown out. The meeting then voted for his motions: that the majority Opposition party would provide the Leader of the Opposition; that the party proceed to elect a leader; and that the leader so chosen be authorized to negotiate a coalition of Opposition forces.[42]

Menzies won the leadership against T. W. White, Spender and Allan McDonald. Amazingly, Hughes not only sought the deputy leadership but won it unanimously notwithstanding that, as Menzies put it, his "qualifications as an up-and-coming understudy to a leader are not obvious. . . . I have as my deputy in the great work of regenerating a Party and enlivening a political Opposition, an old gentleman, all of whose dynamic force is used retrospectively."[43] Hughes's service as deputy leader lasted barely six months.

Menzies' recollections of the very large task confronting him in September 1943 convey the enormity of the assignment:

> . . . I began six years of incessant labour in the study, in the House, and all over Australia. And the labour was incessant. As Leader of a depleted Opposition, I had to carry great burdens in the debating of measures introduced by the Government and in the working out of our own ideas. . . I had to travel inter-state and

address meetings, and "keep the flag flying." This was expensive, not only financially but in terms of nervous energy.[44]

Especially but not only in the *Forgotten People* speeches Menzies had sown the seeds for the new party. For the first time since Federation a leading statesman had expounded ideas, principles and philosophies for what had long been the governing party under a variety of names, Liberal, Nationalist, United Australia. But now the task of manifesting these ideas in an organisation suited for mid-century politics, post-Depression, post-war, was high on the agenda.

This task was both Menzies' burden and his opportunity:

> The one virtue I may claim is that I foresaw that, in the post-war years, Australia would be presented with a choice between a continuation of government control on the Socialist model and a society based upon free and encouraged private enterprise. The latter could not, if social justice was to be achieved, be an irresponsible enterprise. There was to be nothing doctrinaire about our policies.[45]

1944: *a crucial year for Australian politics*

In clearing the way for political revitalisation, Menzies looked beyond the circumstances of the present. He realized that the parliamentary strength of the Government meant that the Opposition could not expect to have much day-to-day impact on the conduct of the war. With his attention increasingly focussed on the post-war world, he soon removed the Opposition from the Advisory War Council. The political rationale for the Council had largely disappeared now that the Government had good majorities in each House; continued Opposition membership simply associated it with government policies and decisions over which it had little influence.

Menzies, in his continuing advocacy of ideas, left no doubt that rejection of socialism, "so dull and sterile," did not mean endorsement of the dogmas of classical economics:

> I will never give a moment's countenance to ideas of laissez-faire, of unrestricted and soulless competition for goods and labour and money, of "each for himself and the devil take the hindmost," nor will the Party I lead. I believe in a man being at liberty to make a good profit or earn a good income, but the profit or income must not be his primary right but his secondary right, always residuary to the discharge of civilised obligations to his employees and his neighbours, the provision of good housing and health services and National Insurance and an enlightened educational structure which opens all doors to the intelligent sons and daughters of underprivileged people.[46]

It was a refrain which would reappear in his speeches. On another occasion: "There is no room in Australia for a party of reaction. There is no useful place for a policy of negation."[47] On 27 May 1944 the opposition forces in New South Wales were very soundly defeated by the Labor Government which had come back to office in 1941. The UAP actually fell apart as polling day approached, replaced by the Liberal Democratic Party and what called itself the Democratic Party; the former won no seats, the latter 12. It was an unusually clear demonstration that in politics, disunity is death.

More encouraging to the Opposition was a Commonwealth referendum on 19 August 1944 on post-war reconstruction and democratic rights, often referred to as the "powers" referendum, embracing among other things civil aviation, uniformity of railway gauges, price control, organized marketing, and national health.

Menzies campaigned with his usual vigour and the referendum was decisively rejected; it was only in South Australia and Western Australia that there were affirmative majorities.

Significantly in the larger scene, on 16 June 1944, Menzies convened a meeting in Melbourne of UAP "Parliamentary Party Leaders and Office Bearers in all States" to discuss the campaign against the referendum proposal. In a statement issued at the end of the meeting Menzies said:

> Delegates to the Conference expressed the opinion at its conclusion that it had been of great value in cementing the relationships between the various State organisations. It was the first full interstate conference that had been held for some time and the agreement shown during the discussion was an indication of strong unity of feeling, both on the referendum and on political questions generally.[48]

In Menzies' view, the result strengthened his position. It also gave authority to his invitation:

> to all non-Labour bodies (other than the Country Party, with which we can always negotiate later on) to attend a conference in Canberra in about a month's time to have a shot at setting up an Australia-wide organization with a Federal Executive and Secretariat and proper equipment for conducting a national campaign.[49]

In his letter Menzies convening the Canberra conference, Menzies wrote:

> The time seems opportune for an effort to secure unity of
> action and organisation among political groups which
> stand for a liberal, progressive policy and are opposed
> to Socialism with its bureaucratic administration and
> restriction of personal freedom.[50]

Thus, on 13 October 1944, leading parliamentary figures, Commonwealth and State, joined representatives of the Australian Women's National League (Victoria and Tasmania), the Queensland Women's Electoral League, the Institute of Public Affairs (NSW and Victoria), the Australian Constitutional League (Victoria, Tasmania, Western Australia), the Democratic Party (NSW), the Liberal Democratic Party of Australia (NSW), the Liberal and Country League (SA), the Kooyong Citizens' Association (Victoria), the Country-National Organization of Queensland, the United Australia Organization, Victoria, the Nationalist Party (Victoria), the Services and Citizen's Party (Victoria), the United Australia and Nationalist Organisation of Tasmania, and the National Party of Western Australia and United Australia Party (Fed). There were 77 delegates and observers altogether.

In the three days of its meetings the conference, working through committees, came up with two main recommendations for the various organisations to consider and, if in agreement, adopt.

First, there was the matter of the party's name. In addition to traditional names that had been used from time to time, there were a number of others such as: Commonwealth; Unionist; Constitutionalist; Conservative; and Progressive. But Liberal Party of Australia, with a long pedigree in Australian politics, was preferred. Menzies later explained:

> When, therefore, we decided to call the new and united

party the Liberal Party, we were adopting no analogy
to the Liberal Party in the United Kingdom. On the
contrary, we were aiming at political progress and
power in our own right. We took the name "Liberal"
because we were determined to be a progressive party,
willing to make experiments, in no sense reactionary
but believing in the individual, his rights, and his
enterprise, and rejecting the Socialist panacea.[51]

The second committee offered proposals about the party's
constitution and organization. It covered the relationship
between the federal organization and State branches; and
between parliamentarians and the party organisation.

Questions of principles, philosophy and policy were naturally
on the agenda. These encompassed much that Menzies had
been speaking about in his radio broadcasts; in this context,
with the war's end in sight, there was much emphasis on
defence matters, and the veterans of the war. As usual, the
significance of the individual, "the prime motive force for
building a better world," was stressed.

Menzies, in his closing address, quoted from a Victorian
IPA publication, *Looking Forward*. Its orientation was
to the economic responsibilities of the state in tackling
unemployment; standards of living, encouraging the
enterprise and resourcefulness of individuals and groups,
and preservation of those natural resources essential to life
and future prosperity.

Ian Hancock commented: "By endorsing the Victorian IPA's
conception of a role for the state, and of the partnership
between the state and private enterprise, Menzies again
explicitly rejected the pre-war economic thinking which was
still current within the New South Wales IPA."[52]

"The Canberra conference," Hancock wrote, "formed an intention, not a political party".[53] Menzies summed up its accomplishment thus: "the Canberra Conference not only declared for unity, but decided on a name and on broadly-stated objectives."[54]

Two months later, a conference at Albury, 14-18 December, set about taking creation of the new party to its next stage. The choice of Albury was symbolic, to counter any impression that the new party was essentially metropolitan; and convenient: "travel," Menzies wrote, "has become so difficult that it is worthwhile selecting a place which will save all the delegates from Victoria, Tasmania, South Australia and Western Australia, an extra night sitting up on the train."[55]

Hancock, in his account, wrote:

> The conference accepted a number of organisational principles recommended by its committees: maximum autonomy for the States; a federal body to co-ordinate State activities "and to afford a means of expression to an all-Australia Party"; a federal secretariat for co-ordination, research and publicity, and to assist the federal parliamentary party; elected State and federal councils and branches; State and federal joint standing committees on policy, with equal representation of parliamentary and non-parliamentary members and chaired by the respective parliamentary leader; the party "would raise and control its own funds . . . [and] would be free of any possibility of control from outside itself and determine its own destiny."[56]

Menzies himself underlined some key principles upon which the Party was founded:

> . . . the twin ideas of Organization control of the Platform and

Parliamentary Party control of Election policy within the broad principles of the Platform . . . were established.[57]

The Albury decisions also put financing the Party on a clearly principled basis. Menzies succinctly stated: "It must be made evident that we were not [the servants of] 'Big Business;' it must be expressly clear that the new Party organization would raise and control its own finances. This was done."[58]

The Liberals left Albury with a Provisional Federal Executive, a draft constitution, a vague set of principles, and boundless enthusiasm.[59] An *Argus* journalist put it neatly: the Liberal Party at this stage really consisted of a commander in chief and the nucleus of a general staff. An army had still to be "recruited, drilled and enthused for a decisive battle within about eighteen months against a strongly entrenched political enemy."[60]

The progress was nevertheless considerable and it is not surprising that two decades later Menzies would write:

> It was quite plain that 1944 was a crucial year for Australian politics. Labour had just had a smashing victory, and the Opposition, in the country though not in the House, was dejected and divided. Labour could afford to look to the future with great Socialist hopes. . . . If things were allowed to settle down into a continuance of this political pattern, Labour's future would be bright, and that of its opponents shadowy indeed. . . .
>
> In 1944, it was clear that my main task, as Leader of the Opposition, was to secure the organic and mental unity of fourteen fractions. This, of course, was far more than a problem of mechanics. . . . It was therefore necessary for me, as the promoter, to prepare the foundations for

a comprehensive statement of political objectives.[61]

This was sufficiently accomplished at Albury for Menzies, in February 1945, to rise in the House of Representatives and say:

> I have to announce that, in consequence of the formation of the Liberal Party of Australia, those who sit with me in this House desire to be known in future as members of the Liberal Party.[62]

As it happened, the new Party had had its first electoral success only a few weeks earlier, in a by-election for the State seat of Ryde (NSW), held on 3 February 1945.

The 1946 election

Much had to be done in the field and 1945 was a year of great activity. Hancock summed it up:

> Within nine months they managed to launch six State divisions, approve and implement a federal constitution, hold an inaugural federal council and elect a federal executive, form nearly 800 branches and enrol some 100 000 members, establish and finance the Federal Secretariat and, on 31 August 1945, formally launch the Liberal Party of Australia.[63]

Early in the election year, 1946, the Party adopted, for the first time, a "Federal Platform." "We declared," Menzies wrote, "that we wanted to have an Australian Nation

> In which an intelligent, free, and liberal Australian democracy shall be maintained by
>
> (a)   Parliament controlling the Executive and the Law controlling all;

(b)   Freedom of speech, religion, and association;

(c)   Freedom of citizens to choose their own way of life, subject to the rights of others;

(d)   Protecting the people against exploitation;

(e)   Looking primarily to the encouragement of individual initiative and enterprise as the dynamic force of reconstruction and progress.[64]

The result of the 1946 election was disappointing for the new Party but also encouraging. Labor won 43 seats in the House of Representatives, a loss of six. The Liberals and the Country Party each took two seats from Labor; Jack Lang won a seat in New South Wales and Mrs Doris Blackburn, widow of Maurice, won his old seat of Bourke in Victoria.

In the Senate, Labor did not quite match its clean sweep of 1943. But winning 15 of the 18 seats contested, it now had 33 of the 36 seats. Only Queensland had gone against the trend and its three victorious senators, one Country Party, the others Liberal, included Annabel Rankin, the first woman from the Party to become a senator.

In terms of voting percentages, the results in 1943 and 1946 were, as Gerard Henderson has pointed out, similar, but with a very important exception. In 1943 12.2 per cent of non-Labor voting supported various independent candidates; in 1946, that support had transferred to the unified Liberal Party.[65]

Menzies reflected on the 1946 result:

> Our organization was relatively new; there were still some teething troubles. It was not reasonable to expect to win the many seats that would be needed to put the Government out. We won a few seats, and were unlucky

not to win a few more. As I wrote to Arthur Fadden shortly afterwards: "When you consider that the task was to arrest the momentum of Labour, and then to secure some movement in the opposite direction, the result of the election is not unsatisfactory."

I might have added, in the old French aphorism, that "it is the first step that counts."[66]

In terms of dispositions, there was much truth in Menzies' claim that "[a]lthough the people did not accept [the Liberal's 'truly post-war policy'] to the extent of turning the government out, we emphasised post-war thinking and progressive ideas, while Labor dwelt rather heavily and sluggishly on the past."[67] This contrast would be far more marked in the next election.

On the day of the election there were referendums on three proposals to alter the Constitution, concerning social services, organised marketing of primary products and industrial employment. All proposals entailed vesting greater powers in the Commonwealth.[68]

Each proposal won a majority of the nation-wide vote - 54.39 percent; 50.57 percent and 50.30 percent respectively - but only that concerning social services secured the necessary State majorities (all six States). The other two questions were supported by majorities in New South Wales, Victoria and Western Australia only.

The scene in the States

Party fortunes in the States give a useful impression of the the various situations of the parties. Within little more than a year of the 1946 Federal election there were elections in all the States. The predominance Labor had enjoyed since 1943, where it was in office everywhere except in South Australia, no longer held, but the victories of the Liberal side, in Western Australia and Victoria, were tenuous.

Incumbent Labor governments retained office comfortably in Queensland, New South Wales and Tasmania. In New South Wales there was a very small swing to Labor. The Country Party vote fell slightly. The Liberal vote rose by more than 10 percent, repeating the pattern noted by Henderson in the Federal election.

In Queensland, Labor's vote fell by less than one percent; votes for its opponents increased by a similarly small margin.

The Liberal Country League survived in South Australia but its vote fell by nearly seven percent while Labor's went up from 42.50 percent to 48.60 percent.

The new Liberal Party was successful in both Western Australia and Victoria. Its vote rose by 12 percent in Western Australia; Labor's fell by nearly seven percent. The McLarty Government won a second term in 1950 but was defeated in 1953, a year in which Coalition fortunes, while improving from the previous year, were nonetheless low, a result of economic problems arising from the Korean War.

The Victorian election of November 1947 brought a Liberal-Country Party coalition to office for little more than a year. Thereafter the Liberals governed alone, but with Country Party support. Following an election in 1950, the Liberal Party government was replaced after much negotiation by a Country Party ministry. Until the next election, the spoils of office rotated between a breakaway group of Liberals and the Country Party. In the subsequent election of 1952, Labor for the first time won a majority in the Legislative Assembly.

Settling the new Party

In the months after the election the Party continued to develop, to recruit that army of which the *Argus* had written in the wake of the Albury conference. By 30 June 1947 there were more than a thousand branches with upwards of 100 000 members. Both branches and members were spread between metropolitan and country areas. Its advantages in contrast to Labor included emphasis on encouraging youth and acceptance and promotion of women.[69]

A big advantage lay in the Party's own organisation. Unlike its predecessors the Party had a capable national staff in the Federal Secretariat led, in the first instance, by Donald Cleland, a brigadier during the war and subsequently Administrator of the Territory of Papua and New Guinea for a decade and a half.

In addition to establishing the Party's institutional structures federally and in each State, the Liberals assembled "a community of skilled and shrewd administrators."[70] Principal among these were John Carrick in New South Wales, a former prisoner-of-war recruited in 1946 as a research officer and appointed General Secretary of the division at the end of 1947[71]; and John Mc Connell, also an ex-serviceman, appointed general secretary in Victoria in August 1945.

Carrick, especially, was an adherent of the view that the business of winning elections began well before polling day: his precept was that you can't fatten the pig on market day. An early illustration of the Party's innovations in campaigning was the John Henry Austral series of 15-minute radio plays which ran twice-weekly between April 1947 and December 1948 on more than 80 commercial stations around Australia. The episodes lampooned Chifley and the Labor Government.

> In all, there were 200 episodes, spanning a twenty-month season. In each episode, "John Henry" would explore, emotively, an everyday topic and, with what was described as "good humoured ruthlessness", would castigate Labor's bureaucratic and socialist policies. It was skilful softening up for the more orthodox campaigning closer to polling day.[72]

A comparable venture, the "Country Quiz," "sought to woo rural listeners by combining technical information and entertainment. Each quiz session concluded with the announcement that it was offered as a 'gesture of friendship and goodwill by Liberal supporters throughout the country,' who understood the need to increase primary production and who wanted to assist 'the man on the land' to enjoy a greater measure of prosperity."[73]

The initiatives symbolised the Party's innovative cam-paigning which was strengthened by astute use of polling (then in its infancy as a tool in politics) and employment of commercial advertisers, the Hansen-Rubensohn Company, in 1947 (the company had previously been used by Labor). What Richard Casey, the Federal President, was looking for was, as Hancock put it, "aggressive, persistent and profes-sional advertising."[74]

The Party's greatest strength was what Hancock appropriately described as "the revived enthusiasm of thousands of ordinary members and their leaders across Australia who believed that socialism would destroy all that was good in their country."[75]

Nothing did more to revive that enthusiasm than Prime Minister Chifley's announcement, in a press statement on Saturday 16 August 1947 of 40 or so words, after a meeting of the ministry throughout day, that:

> Cabinet today authorised the Attorney General, Dr Evatt, and myself to prepare legislation for submission to the Federal Parliamentary Labor Party for nationalisation of banking, other than State banks, with proper protection for shareholders, depositors, borrowers and staffs of private banks.[76]

"That was it in its grossly inadequate wholeness," according to Gerard Henderson. He continued: "There was no clarifying statement or comment for a full month."[77]

Almost immediately there was active public hostility to the decision. In little more than a week (25 August) the Liberal Party organised a meeting at the Sydney Town Hall; it attracted an overflow audience. The pace of events is well-captured by Allan Martin:

> Apathy was not, however, a problem in the earliest days after Chifley's bank nationalization move. In Canberra the Labor Caucus formally approved the idea at a meeting on 16 September. By then formidable agitation against nationalization was already under way. Two days earlier, for example, the United Bank Officers' Association in Sydney gathered a crowd estimated by police at 10 000 at a protest meeting in the Domain, and officials set out for Canberra by car with petitions containing "hundreds of thousands of signatures against the nationalisation plan" and determined to interview every member of Caucus. On the night when the Labor Caucus made its decision Casey, as Federal President of the Liberal Party, spoke

in protest on eighty-eight commercial radio stations, and next day addressed a lunchtime audience of 3 000 in the Sydney Town Hall . . . When parliament resumed a few days later, Menzies launched a censure motion denouncing the Government for its "tyranny", accusing it of lacking a mandate and demanding a referendum on bank nationalization. Chifley replied that suggestions of totalitarianism were absurd. There could be no dictatorship in a parliament that had to face the electors every three years. The people, in the Constitution, had given the Commonwealth parliament complete power if it thought it appropriate to legislate over banking.[78]

"From August 1947," Henderson tellingly observes, "Robert Menzies had a cause. Now, at last, some reality could be grafted on to the familiar Liberal rhetoric of the 'socialistic Labor vs individualist Liberals' variety."[79]

To Menzies himself, "The issue of Socialism was no longer academic. It came alive, and the critics subsided."[80]

The legislation had no trouble passing either the House of Representatives or the Senate. But, in addition to the public activity it occasioned in the electorate, it remained in the public eye. Before there was any action to implement the scheme, it was held invalid by the High Court of Australia in 1948. The following year, with the election fast approaching, the Judicial Committee of the Privy Council rejected the Government's attempt to have the High Court's decision overruled.

Referendums, parliamentary broadcasting, electoral redistribution and Senate reform.

In its very formative years the Liberal Party derived significant benefit from various referendums sponsored by the Curtin and then the Chifley governments. In 1944 and 1948 they furnished opportunities for building popular and voting support in real situations where the fate of the government was not at stake. The 1944 powers referendum provided Menzies with his first chance to bring the parliamentary leaders of the UAP together. The referendum fared badly. Three referendums were held in conjunction with the September 1946 Federal election; two failed; one which empowered the Commonwealth to adopt various social service programs, was passed.

Another referendum, in May 1948, to authorise the Commonwealth to continue to use war-time powers to control rents and prices, was heavily defeated and not supported in any State. The Liberal Party's organisation had been usefully tested in an actual contest which fitted well with general themes about the need to end war-time restrictions and curtail growing centralisation in the nation.

R. G. Casey, Federal President of the Party, hailed the "no" vote as heralding a new political era in Australia: "The battleground has changed," he claimed. "A gigantic struggle between Socialism and free enterprise has now supplanted the old fight between Labour and Liberal."[81]

Broadcasting of parliamentary proceedings started in 1946. It gave Menzies a new avenue for deploying his proven skills on radio. He believed it gave an advantage to the Opposition:

. . . politically, it proved to be a Government mistake

> [he wrote]. Those citizens who "listened in" – and, except on a few extraordinary occasions, they were a small minority – were fascinated by the attack, and somewhat uninterested in the defence. So, on the air, we, the Opposition, made headway.[82]

It certainly meant that when, on Thursday 23 October 1947, Menzies rose to lead the attack on the bank nationalisation legislation in one of his most notable speeches, he was not only able to speak to the House of Representatives, whose galleries were full to over-flowing, but to the nation as a whole.

In the following year a much more substantial change took place. The Government decided to enlarge the Parliament significantly, for the first time since establishment of the Commonwealth. The House was increased from 74 to 121 (and, in addition, two seats with limited voting rights representing the Australian Capital Territory and the Northern Territory); and the Senate from 36 to 60. Moreover, the method of electing Senators was changed from a winner-take-all formula to proportional representation.

Curiously, Chifley had not said anything about this in his policy speech for the 1946 election. Menzies, on the other hand, had been quite specific. On the question of the size of the Parliament, he had said:

> . . . an effective democracy requires that Parliament should be fully representative, that Members should not be so immersed in matters of detail as to be unable to devote full consideration to major matters of policy, and that there should be the widest possible area of choice of the Ministers who have to accept the ultimate responsibility of administration.[83]

On the question of electing Senators, he considered that:

> . . . the present system under which all the candidates
> elected in any one State are inevitably of one side of
> politics is basically unsatisfactory. . . . we believe that
> an early attempt must be made to devise some new
> method of Senate election and some way of making
> the introduction of the new method fair to both sides
> of politics, and to electors of all shades of political
> opinion.[84]

The most predictable of these changes was in the Senate. Under proportional representation there was no prospect of a Coalition majority in the Senate, irrespective of what might happen in the House of Representatives; the very best it could hope for was 27 seats, four short of a majority. [In the event, as shall be shown, the outcome of what Menzies later called "a scandalous manoeuvre"[85] was 26 seats to the Coalition (Government), 34 to Labor (Opposition).]

Menzies also understood that under the new voting system a double dissolution would be a much less certain means of resolving differences between the Houses. In any election for the full Senate in the days before minor parties and independents started to win places there, the probability would be equal numbers in a new Senate, the dispute would thus need to be resolved in a joint sitting of the two Houses. (Indeed, the Senate result in the double dissolution election of 1951 is one of the few occasions when a Government has secured majorities in both Houses since these changes.)

The Federal Election, 10 December 1949

In June 1948 Menzies sailed for Britain, accompanied by wife Pattie and daughter Heather. They spent most of the time in England but visited also Scotland. He himself went to the United States when the presidential campaigns of that year were at their most intense, and Canada. The visit reflected his recognition that, important as was administration domestically, government was also about overseeing Australia's place in the international community and fostering relations with those nations important to it for reasons of trade as well as defence and security. Questions of international security at this time were very much influenced by the Berlin blockade which began just a few weeks before his arrival in Europe.

The trip aroused a certain amount of curiosity, not least among gossip columnists, but, for Menzies, the reason was straightforward: *"This* is to be a refresher course for me spiritually, mentally and physically, and I hope to come back 'fighting fit'."[86]

He returned to Australia in the first week of 1949 and immediately resumed an extensive program of speaking throughout Australia as well as in Parliament. His travels within Australia conspicuously included industrial and other centres "not usually regarded as Liberal strongholds."[87] He also gave a series of broadcasts, "The Liberal Leader Speaks".

With bank nationalisation now before the Judicial Committee of the Privy Council, to whom the Government had appealed after the High Court declared the legislation unconstitutional, the big questions of domestic politics were industrial unrest, especially instigated by the Miners' Union, the Federated Ironworkers' Union and the Waterside Workers' Federation, all with prominent communist leadership. His visits were often well-received, but not always.

Strikes in the mines in New South Wales led the Chifley

Government to send in the Army. Meanwhile, Lance Sharkey, general secretary of the Communist Party, was jailed for uttering seditious words. Combined with the Soviet announcement that it had the atomic bomb, tensions in Eastern Europe, over Czechoslovakia as well as Berlin, and the imminent victory of communist forces in China meant that the Coalition's anti-communist campaigning, including plans for secret ballots in unions and the undertaking to ban the Communist Party (not personally supported by Menzies[88]), had a very receptive audience.

On the eve of the election, the Government reimposed petrol rationing. Highlighting the Government's post-war reconstruction initiatives, the Snowy Mountains Hydro-Electric project was officially opened with a certain amount of grumbling by the Liberal Deputy Premier of Victoria, Wilfrid Kent Hughes, now seeking a seat in the House of Representatives, that little credit had been given to Victoria for its role and that all speakers were Labor. There was no comparable controversy when, a week later, the foundation stone of the Australian National University was laid.

The Parliament was dissolved on 31 October. Menzies opened the Coalition campaign at Canterbury Town Hall in his electorate of Kooyong on 10 November. The leader of the Country Party, Fadden, sat on the platform, the first time coalition partners had come together in such a manner since the Country Party's foundation after the Great War, thus underlining the unity of the two parties confronting Labor. Menzies himself would be on the platform when Fadden delivered the Country Party's policy speech in Boonah a week later.

Menzies' big theme was the contest between advocates of

the Socialist State and those of individualism and enterprise. He contrasted Labor of 1946 with Labor in 1949:

> In 1946 you could vote Labour, reasonably supposing that it was a party of reform and not of socialisation. In 1949 it is clear that a Labour vote is for the socialist objective and for nothing else.[89]

He also went to considerable lengths to assure voters that the Coalition stood for full employment, reminding them that a Labor government was not a guarantee against unemployment. Another preoccupation was a constructive attitude to industrial relations:

> The highest production and living standards cannot be achieved without a new and human spirit in the industrial world. No industry can succeed without the cooperation of capital, management and labour. Each must be encouraged. Each must be fairly rewarded. Between the three there must be mutual understanding and respect.[90]

Chifley's policy speech was pre-recorded and shorter than Menzies': he stood by the Government's record, expressly eschewing "bribing the electors"!

The major metropolitan papers were generally friendly to the Coalition. The *Sydney Morning Herald* thought that Menzies had been "trenchant and forthright" while *The Age* thought it a "bold challenge on socialisation." On the Coalition side, Fadden seemed to be the main target of criticism. *The Age* wrote that his account of the issues which the electors must decide was "so grossly over-coloured as to invite derision."[91]

Menzies campaigned with all his usual energy notwithstanding a bout of flu late in November. He visited all States except, owing to his indisposition, Western Australia.

As the campaign progressed he developed considerable momentum notwithstanding, but faced some bitter attacks from some opponents anxious to revive hostilities with "Pig-Iron" Bob.

His skills on the hustings were not lost on a staff reporter on the *Sydney Morning Herald*: there would be, ran the report on Monday 12 December, "red faces" among Liberal supporters who once maintained that Menzies was "an election liability and a political 'has been'." Menzies was in fact the Opposition's "No. 1 Drawcard."[92]

The Coalition vote jumped by nearly eight percent whilst Labor's fell by nearly four percent; the Liberal Party share itself rose by more than 10 percent. The Coalition emerged from the election with 74 seats, a majority of 26 over Labor. Thus, notwithstanding the enlargement of the House by 47 seats, Labor managed only to increase its numbers by 5; the Coalition added 45 seats.

As was expected, it was a different story in the Senate. It is around the Senate result that the next and final episode of this account revolves.

In the meantime, the fourth Menzies Government took office. Despite more than eight years in opposition, and the massive defeat in 1943, most of the 19 ministers had figured in the coalition governments of the late 1930s and leading up to October 1941. Among the old warriors, Hughes stayed on the backbench, this time until his death! But Page again took a place at the Cabinet table. Casey had returned from his international sojourns in Washington, Cairo and Calcutta; various Senators had recovered their places, in the case of Philip McBride by returning to the House. Dame Enid Lyons, Vice-President of the Executive Council, became the first woman appointed to a ministry; she was also the only Tasmanian.

The newcomers to ministerial office were Senator Neil O'Sullivan (Qld), Leader of the Government in the Senate; Josiah Francis (Qld); Senator William Spooner, a formidable figure in the Party's New South Wales Branch (and brother of Eric Spooner, a leading intriguer against Menzies in 1941); Senator Cooper (Qld); and Howard Beale (NSW), elected in 1946.

Among the heavy-weights, Victoria was well-represented not only by Menzies and Holt, but by White and Senator John Spicer as well, and by McEwen from the Country Party. New South Wales, by contrast, could boast Harrison, Spender, Spooner and Beale among Liberal ministers and Page and H. L. Anthony from the Country Party. Fadden, O'Sullivan, Josiah Francis and Walter Cooper came from Queensland. Two South Australians, Senator George McLeay and Philip McBride, completed the team. There was no-one from Western Australia. (In the previous parliament, 1946-49, all Western Australian places, House and Senate, had been held by the Labor Party with the sole exception of a single Country Party member.)

Epilogue

Great as the victory had been, Menzies was well aware that Labor's strength in the Senate, 34 seats to the Coalition's 26, meant that the new government was hardly entrenched. Menzies' own experience of politics would have been sufficient to alert him to the precariousness of this situation. He was old enough to recall the double dissolution of 1914.

It was brought on by the Liberal prime minister of the time, Joseph Cook, in response Labor's deployment of its Senate numbers (31-5) to hassle a ministry with only a one-seat majority in the House; Menzies may even have recalled Cook's very direct tactics in Parliament in contriving the first use of the double dissolution provision of the Constitution (section 57). Whatever his recollections of 1913-14, he was certainly deeply conscious of the Senate's role in the fate of the Scullin Government, 1930-31, notwithstanding that Scullin resisted suggestions that he seek a double dissolution. Moreover, few understood the implications of election of senators by proportional voting, especially for a new government, when it was introduced in 1948, as clearly as Menzies did.

At the time, Labor was circumspect. Its attitude in 1948 had been that, whatever happened in the House of Representatives, its strength in the Senate was impregnable and would enable it to defend the Curtin-Chifley legacy, at least for the first term of any Coalition government.

As in 1913-14, there was no talk within Labor circles of respecting the mandate of a ministry with a substantial and recent majority in the House of Representatives. Nor did the approach adopted by the Conservative Party in the House of Lords after Labour's big win in the House of Commons in 1945 have any resonance in Canberra; the House of Lords was a hereditary chamber whereas the Senate was a body elected on the same franchise as the House of Representatives.

In the ordinary course of events, the next election for the House would not need to be held until early 1953, with the probability that it would be held late in 1952, that is, three years after the previous election. New Senate terms would not start until 1 July 1953, so election of senators could be held at any time after 1 July 1952. The probability would again be that the two elections would be held simultaneously as had hitherto invariably been the case.

There was thus plenty of time for Labor to haggle over the Government's legislative program. There remained, however, a strong possibility that the expedient course was a double dissolution. It was true that delays could have dangerous ends; a double dissolution was, thus, at once the boldest and the riskiest course.

And it is the one which Menzies eventually took. He eschewed, however, Cook's approach of a contrivance, relying instead on legislation deriving directly from the Government's mandate. Initially the Communist Party Dissolution Bill appeared to be the most likely legislation upon which to base a double dissolution. Labor eventually swung behind the Government and the legislation passed (it was subsequently challenged successfully in the High Court; a consequential attempt to have the legislation enacted by means of an amendment to the Constitution failed at referendum).

Other major legislation of the Government systematically challenged by Labor concerned banking, including reinstatement of a board. When it arrived in the Senate on its second consideration by the Parliament, early in 1951, Labor again set about a prolonged examination of the Bill in much the same manner as had occurred in the previous year.

Menzies lost no time in securing a double dissolution on grounds of "failure to pass" and the voters returned to the polls on 28 April, this time to vote both for the House of

Representatives and for the entire Senate. The Coalition vote fell slightly; Labor's increased by 1.65 percent.

But what counted was the seats tally. In the House the Coalition's numbers dropped from 74 to 69; Labor's rose from 48 to 54. The Government thus emerged with a smaller but still very healthy majority of 15.

It was in the Senate that the Coalition reaped its real reward. Its numbers rose from 26 to 32; Labor's fell from 34 to 28. For the first time in 11 years the Coalition had good majorities in both Houses, quite a feat under the new proportional voting system for the Senate. The comeback from 1940-43, the Slough of Despond, was now complete.

Menzies' achievement

It is not enough to appraise the combined results of 1949 and 1951 as the measure of the Coalition's recovery nor of Menzies' new, very convincing ascendancy in Australia's national politics. Even reviewing his record in the next 15 years, with another five triumphs in the House and a generally secure situation in the Senate, albeit not invariably with a majority, does only partial justice.

A better measure of his accomplishment, from relinquishing UAP leadership in 1941 to consolidation of the Coalition return to power under his leadership in 1951, lies in the new unity and order he had fostered among the assorted forces of Liberalism in this decade.

The Menzies' initiatives of 1944-45 were the fourth effort at unity by the non-Labor side. The previous three – embodied in the fusion of Protectionist and (Anti-Socialist) Free Trade groups in 1909; formation of the Nationalist Party in 1917; and of the United Australia Party in 1931 – were essentially parliamentary re-alignments heavily influenced by the configuration of parties in the House of Representatives. The first was a merger. The second and third efforts were occasioned by splits in the Labor Party and the need to accommodate those members who had left Labor.

In 1909 the merger led immediately to defeat of the Fisher Labor Government and its replacement by the merged party led by Alfred Deakin as prime minister. This new combination was defeated in both the House and the Senate at the 1910 election. The 1917 combination saw the joining of the then Commonwealth Liberal Party led by Joseph Cook with the rump National Labor Government led by Hughes. The new entity, the Nationalist Party, took office in February 1917. Elections were held in May and the new ministry won by 53 seats to Labor's 22, 20 fewer than the 42 seats it had won at the previous election.

In 1931, defectors from the Scullin Labor Government joined with the Nationalist Opposition in the United Australia Party; Joe Lyons, one of the defectors, became the leader, brought on defeat of the Scullin Government in the House and subsequently led the United Australia Party to victory in national elections in December.

As in the case of the 1909 merger, there were electoral and organisational consequences of the parliamentary realignments in both 1917 and 1931-2. There was not, however, any real effort to develop a formal institutional structure broadly based in the electorate.

Nor was anything done in these three instances to put party financing on a proper basis; Menzies wrote that the

UAP, "except for a very nominal membership fee, had been financed by special and largely self-appointed bodies" who, in New South Wales, "did not hesitate to say what policies should be pursued."[93]

There were changes in the electorates but these were consequential upon the parliamentary developments. There was some organisational reorganisation but rarely to the extent of framing a constitution, regularising financial arrangements or putting the new parliamentary party on either a popular or an Australia-wide basis.

In none of these cases did the leaders of the new parties, Deakin, Hughes, then Bruce, nor Lyons, make any dedicated effort to formulate, articulate and advocate philosophies and principles for the party beyond that which was incidental to speeches in Parliament and campaigning. Hughes certainly never did for the Nationalist Party what he had done for Labor with *The Case for Labor* (1910).[94]

The formation of the Liberal Party was markedly different in all these respects. At the parliamentary level it was not a merger, nor was it about accommodating exiles from some other group. It was directed much more to united organisation for the purpose of contesting elections; it was about addressing the dispersal of forces which had been so damaging in the 1943 election.

There was great priority to giving the new Party clear institutional form and this meant a constitution with Australia-wide application. And the constitutions devised, at both national and state levels, provided for membership involvement, especially of women, in a structured manner in the governance of the party.

The financing of the Party received special attention: "the new Party organization would raise and control its own finances."[95]

And the Party had both a philosophy, in which *The Forgotten People* had a special place, and a leader, a gifted orator, who knew the significance of principle and policy in fighting the political battle.

What Menzies had accomplished was largely unprecedented elsewhere. The Conservative Party in Britain, following its defeat in 1945, had taken some important measures. It had set up a research department; it had greatly enhanced its financial arrangements under Lord Woolton. But it gave little attention to its approach to government. Some if its members had made contributions, of which Harold Macmillan's *The Middle Way* and Quinton Hogg's *The Case for Conservatism* have proven to be the most durable.[96] But they were not effective matches for the continuing efforts on behalf of Labour by Richard Crossman and Anthony Crosland.

Counterpart parties elsewhere had likewise largely confined renewed efforts to challenge the collectivism resulting from the Depression and the Second World War to new electoral techniques, polling, advertising and travel.

Thus, as the 1949 election approached, Liberalism in Australia was unusually well-placed not simply to fight an election in the usual manner, with a considerable measure of modernisation. It had a refreshed philosophy attuned to the debates of the post-war world; advocacy was central to its campaigning (and an advocate in the top rank of parliamentary orators); and it had recreated itself organisationally and financially on an Australia-wide basis.

That was the essential and very considerable accomplishment of Menzies and all those who joined with him, in Parliament and in the community, not only for the battle of 1949 and its aftermath early in 1951, but for the next decade and a half.

Notes

1   Cited A. W. Martin, *Robert Menzies: a Life*, volume 2, Melbourne University Press, 1999, 116 [hereafter, Martin, vol 2].

2   Robert Menzies, *The Forgotten People and Other Studies in Democracy*, Melbourne, (1943) 2011, Liberal Party of Australia (Victorian Division).

3   Michael King, *The Penguin History of New Zealand*, Penguin, 2003, 420-21.

4   Heather Henderson (ed.), *Letters to my Daughter: Robert Menzies, letters, 1955-75*, Pier 9, 2001, 85 [letter of 15 January 1962].

5   John Howard, *The Menzies Era: the Years that shaped modern Australia*, HarperCollins, 2014, 58 [hereafter: Howard, *Menzies Era*].

6   Sir Robert Menzies, *Afternoon Light: some memories of men and events*, Cassell Australia, 1967, 56 [hereafter, Menzies, *Afternoon Light*].

7   For Menzies' first prime ministership, see Anne Henderson, *Menzies at War*, NewSouth, 2014; see also, Anne Henderson, "Robert Menzies – War and Peace", J. R. Nethercote (ed.), *Menzies: the Shaping of Modern Australia*, Connor Court, 27-42.

8   Menzies, *Afternoon Light*, 13.

9   Menzies, *Afternoon Light*, 14.

10   Menzies, *Afternoon Light*, 14.

11   Menzies, *Afternoon Light*, 18. On the air disaster, see also Cameron Hazlehurst, *Ten Journeys to Cameron's Farm: an Australian tragedy*, ANU E Press, 2013; and Andrew Tink, *Air Disaster Canberra*, New South Publishing, 2013.

12   Not least by Menzies himself: Menzies, *Afternoon Light*, 19.

13   A. W. Martin, *Robert Menzies, A Life*, volume 1, Melbourne University Press, 1993, 376 [hereafter, Martin, vol 1].

14   Martin, vol 1, 379.

15   Menzies, *Afternoon Light*, 56.

16   Menzies, *Afternoon Light*, 56.

17   Menzies, *Afternoon Light*, 56.

18   Menzies, *Afternoon Light*, 56.

19   Menzies, *Afternoon Light*, 60.

20   Menzies, *Afternoon Light*, 60-61.

21   Martin, vol 1, 397-8.

22   Martin, vol 1, 397-98.

23   Citations from "the Forgotten People" are from Graeme Starr (ed.), *The Liberal Party of Australia; a Documentary History*, Drummond/Heinemann, 1980, 57-63 [hereafter, Starr, *Documentary History*).

24   Joint Opposition Policy, 10 November 1949, Starr, *Documents*, 152.

25   Starr, *Documentary History*, 57-63, 57ff.

26   Howard, *Menzies Era*, 57.

27   Martin, vol 1, 402-03.

28   Martin, vol 1, 398-99.

29   Martin, vol 1, 401.

30   Martin, vol 1, 403-04.

31   Martin, vol 1, 404.

32   Martin, vol 1, 406.

33   Martin, vol 1, 407.

34   Martin, vol 1, 409.

35   Martin, vol 1, 408.

36   Menzies, *Afternoon Light*, 283.

37   Menzies to Ken Menzies, quoted Martin, vol 1, 414-15.

38   Menzies, *Afternoon Light*, 283.

39   See Martin, vol 1, 417.

40   Martin, vol 1, 419.

41   Martin, vol 1, 422.

42   Martin, vol 1, 422.

43   Martin, vol 1, 423.

44   Menzies, *Afternoon Light*, 283.

45   Menzies, *Afternoon Light*, 282.

46   Cited in Ian Hancock, *National and Permanent? The Federal Organisation of the Liberal Party of Australia 1944-1965*, Melbourne University Press, 2000, 23 [Hereafter, Hancock].

47   Hancock, *National and Permanent?*, 31-32.

48   Martin, vol 2, 7.

49   Cited Martin, vol 2, 7.

50   Starr, *Documentary History*, 69.

51   Menzies, *Afternoon Light*, 286.

52   Hancock, 32.

53   Hancock, 34.

54   Menzies, *Afternoon Light*, 290.

55   Martin, vol 2, 11.

56   Hancock, 35.

57   Menzies, *Afternoon Light*, 291.

58   Menzies, *Afternoon Light*, 292; on Party financing, see also Starr, *Documentary History*, 113

59   Hancock, 37.

60   Martin, vol 2, 12.

61   Menzies, *Afternoon Light*, 287.

62   Commonwealth Parliamentary Debates, vol 181, 21 February 1945, 19.

63   Hancock, 37.

64   Menzies, *Afternoon Light*, 292.

65   Gerard Henderson, *Menzies' Child: The Liberal Party of Australia 1994-1994*, Allen & Unwin, 1994, 91 [hereafter Henderson, *Menzies' Child*].

66   Menzies, *Afternoon Light*, 293.

67   Quoted Henderson, *Menzies' Child*, 93, drawing upon Cameron Hazlehurst, *Menzies Observed*, 1979.

68   Geoffrey Sawer, *Australian Federal Politics and Law, 1929-1949*, Melbourne University Press, 1962, 173.

69   Hancock, 81-83.

70   Hancock, 88.

71   See Graeme Starr, *Carrick: Principles, Politics, and Policy*, Connor Court, 2012.

72   Howard, *Menzies Era*, 67.

73   Hancock, 91.

74   Hancock, 90.

75   Hancock, 88

76   Henderson, *Menzies' Child*, 96.

77   Henderson, *Menzies' Child*, 96.

78   Martin, vol 2, 76.

79   Henderson, *Menzies' Child*, 96.

80   Menzies, *Afternoon Light*, 295.

81   Menzies, *Afternoon Light*, 295.

82   Menzies, *Afternoon Light*, 283.

83   Menzies, Policy Speech, 1946.

84   Menzies, Policy Speech, 1946.

85   Joint Government Policy, 1951, cited Starr, *Documentary History*, 166.

86   Martin, vol 2, 86.

87   Martin, vol 2, 104.

88   Menzies, Diary, 22 July 1948, NLA, MS.6936/13/397. Cited Martin, vol 2, 91.

89   Cited Martin, vol 2, 116.

90   Menzies, Policy Speech, 1949.

91   Martin, vol 2, 120.

92   Martin, vol 2, 121.

93   Menzies, *Afternoon Light*, 291.

94   William Morris Hughes, *The Case for Labor*, Sydney University Press, (1910) 1970.

95   Menzies, *Afternoon Light*, 291-92.

96   Harold Macmillan, *The Middle Way*, Macmillan, 1938;Lord Hailsham, *The Case for Conservatism*, Penguin, 1947.

3

The Revival of Liberalism in Australia

Sir Robert Gordon Menzies[2]

This chapter recounts very briefly some of the political events which were subsequent to my election to the leadership of the Opposition in Australia at the end of 1943. It describes the creation of a new party with a modern philosophy, and its ultimate succession to power. If, in this book, I say but little about Australia's political history since 1949, it is not because that history has not been one of problems overcome and in many ways dramatic success, well worth recording, but because of two considerations. The first is that the political history of seventeen years cannot be compressed into a single essay. It will, I hope, be written and documented in broad substance and in close detail by some scholar with the full facilities of research. I cannot attempt so great a task in this book. The second consideration concerns myself. I am still so close to the political events and was so much involved in most of them that, as a still, though fadingly,

---

2   Originally published in *Afternoon Light : some memories of men and events*, Cassell Australia, 1967

controversial figure, I could be found lacking in objectivity. The pulse of party politics has not yet entirely subsided in my blood, though I am happily conscious of an increasing detachment and a more relaxed outlook.

In any case, no man is a good judge in his own cause; that is the great reason why I have no wish to write an autobiography.

But the history of a political movement is a different matter, and I think I should very briefly sketch it.

Strangely enough, as it might appear, I had never, even as a student, been attracted by State Socialism. To me, human beings were individuals, not statistics. And I was an individual, with my own ambitions. From my earliest days until now, I have found 'Socialism' a dreary and essentially reactionary doctrine.

On 6 July 1964, I delivered the first Baillieu Lecture, founded in London in honour of that very great Australian, Lord Baillieu. I made it the occasion for an expression of my own philosophy about Socialism.

> It is frequently charged against those of us who are not Socialists that we are reactionaries; that we want to turn the clock back; that we yearn for a restoration of *laissez-faire*. In the modern world, this is quite untrue. The truth is that it is the non-Socialists who have moved with the times. I can understand, as an intellectual and historical exercise, how Socialism attracted the support of radical thinkers after the industrial revolution in Great Britain, the creation of 'dark satanic mills', the horrors of child labour, when industrial power was in a limited number of hands, when the rights of employed people were either denied or imperfectly recognised, when the infant Trade Unions were too commonly regarded as subversive bodies, when social services as

we now know them were almost non-existent. It is not strange that under these circumstances there grew up in many thoughtful minds the egalitarian belief that the creation of social and industrial justice demanded a high measure of uniformity, and that uniformity could be achieved only by the mastery and management of the State.

But we know, and occasionally admit, that there is no uniformity among personalities, or talents, or energy. We have learned that true rising standards of living are the product of progressive enterprise, the acceptance of risks, the encouragement of adventure, the prospect of rewards. These are all individual matters. There is no Government department which can create these things.

These, though recently expressed, were my views as far back as 1944, when I set about the revival of Liberalism in Australia. The one virtue I may claim is that I foresaw that, in the post-war years, Australia would be presented with a choice between a continuation of government control on the Socialist model and a society based upon free and encouraged private enterprise. The latter could not, if social justice was to be achieved, be an irresponsible enterprise. There was to be nothing doctrinaire about our policies. If I were to become the leader of a great non-Socialist party, I must look at everything in a practical way. My associates and I knew perfectly well that, in Australia at any rate, there have been and are certain elements which, in the very nature of our geography and history, lend themselves to government management or control. Take, for example, the railways, which are for all practical purposes, government-owned and controlled. The development of a young and sparsely populated country would clearly be assisted by the creation of means of transport. New and developmental railway lines would almost certainly begin by operating at a loss; a loss which no private entrepreneur could contemplate. And so, Governments came into the picture, footed the bill, and opened up vast tracts of productive land.

Again, we have for many years lived with government control of postal, telegraphic, and telephonic services. I know that many of these services are in private hands in America; but that has its origins in American history.

But, looking to the future in a rapidly developing country like Australia, it seemed eminently desirable to look more to the citizen and less to government. A great reliance must be made on the creative genius of the individual, assisted, and sometimes controlled by the government in the general social interest, but encouraged and rewarded. The 'profit motive', so vehemently attacked by the Socialists, must be seen as one of the most powerful factors in growth.

The United Australia Party, of which I was a private member at the time of the débâcle of the 1943 General Election, had behind it (more or less) a whole series of unrelated organisations, without cohesion or common purpose.

When we met at Parliament House after the election, the Parliamentary Party at once and unanimously pressed me to resume the leadership. I said that I would do so on two conditions. One was that our party, being the majority opposition party, should assert its right to the Leadership of the Opposition, without which I believed we could not move forward effectively. The other was that I should have *carte blanche* to take all necessary steps toward gathering up all the existing organisations into one Australia-wide organisation, with a new name – the 'United Australia' name having ceased to be up-to-date or self-explanatory – and a carefully prepared platform.

Both of these conditions were agreed to, and I began six years of incessant labour in the study, in the House, and all over Australia. And the labour *was* incessant. As Leader of a depleted Opposition, I had to carry great burdens in the debating of measures introduced by the Government and in the working out of our own ideas. In the Parliamentary recesses I had to travel inter-state and address meetings, and 'keep the flag flying'. This was expensive, not only financially but in terms of nervous energy. The time was to come, under the Menzies Government, where the Leader of the Opposition became entitled to the same emoluments and privileges as a Minister. In my years, I drew a private member's salary, plus an allowance of, I think, £300 a year, and, except on rare official occasions, provided my own transport.

For about a month in each year, I accepted a few briefs, partly to keep my hand in at my own profession, and partly to replenish the domestic larder. In the result, I drew heavily upon my limited private capital.

By October 1944, I convened a meeting of the organisation at the Masonic Hall in Canberra. It interests me very much to read that one non-ranking Junior Senator in the United States has a staff of over sixty. As Leader of the Opposition (and a former Prime Minister) in the National Parliament of Australia, I had a staff of two. All the work which had to be done to convene this meeting was done by myself, with the aid of a devoted Secretary, Miss Eileen Lenihan. I sent out letters to all of the organisations concerned, found favourable responses, and received many valuable suggestions. I felt much encouraged. Clearly, the fields were ready for the sowing, and we could hope for a great harvest. So, with much zest, I completed my preparatory work for a meeting which just had to succeed if we were to have any political significance in the years to come. When the conference met on 13 October 1944, the 'parade state' was as follows. From *New South Wales*, there were the Democratic Party and the Liberal Democratic Party. In *Queensland*, there were the Country National Organisation, the Queensland People's Party (not represented at the Conference, but coming in later, and the Queensland Women's Electoral League. From *Victoria*, there were representatives of the United Australia Organisation, the Australian Women's National League, and the Young Nationalist Organisation (of which I had been one of the founders fifteen years before), the Services and Citizens Party. Another body, the Middle Class Organisation, was not represented, preferring to maintain a non-political character.

South Australia had a single organisation, the Liberal and Country League.

I had with me twelve Members of the Federal Parliament. From each State there were Members of Parliament.

In short, I faced a state of affairs in which I must dedicate myself to bringing fourteen organisations into one, under one banner, and with one body of ideas.

Why had we become so fragmented? The reason is not far to seek. All of the organisations were in opposition, but no doubt for different reasons. Lacking membership of a common body, and the guidance of well-formulated common ideas, we were destined for continued defeat. The Labour Party was in a powerful position to 'divide and conquer'.

As I said at the Canberra Conference, having taken the Chair as Convenor:

The Labour Party, though its policy and administration are repugnant to us, is not something which exists under a different name and with a different set-up in each State. It is the Australian Labour Party. Its membership depends upon common considerations all over the continent. It has State Branches and local branches. It has State executives and a Federal executive. It has all over Australia a system of journals so effective that it has been my experience that the same point of view in almost the same words will be produced by a Labour supporter in Bunbury as by one in Rockhampton.

The result of this unanimity and cohesion on the organisational side has been that the disunities which exist in Labour circles are usually below the surface, are not advertised, and so have nothing like the public effect that is produced by the well-advertised minor differences of opinion that may exist in our own ranks.

When I consider the structure of the Australian Labour Party and realize that the political warfare to which we have been committed for a long time past by no choice of our own is a struggle between political armies, I am driven to wonder how we could ever imagine that a concerted force under one command and with one staff is to be defeated by divided units under separate commands, and with no general staff.

(It must be remembered that those words were spoken before the time, years later, when Labour, in opposition, became deeply divided.)

I set out to inject into the meeting a sense of significance and urgency. If we could not get together then, we might not see success for our political views for many years. There were one or two doubters, who were naturally attached to their own particular groups, but their doubts were soon swept away by the general enthusiasm.

In the upshot, we passed a resolution to say that we would

proceed to form one party, to be known as the Liberal Party of Australia; and that, later in the year, we would have a Special Conference to adopt a Constitution and a Platform.

Why 'Liberal'? This will need explaining to both English and American readers.

The Liberal Party in the United Kingdom is a survival of the great party of Gladstone and Asquith which for so many generations had disputed the field with the Conservative Party. When the Labour Party became, first, a force and then a major force, the Liberal Party became a residual party, destined to be a small group at Westminster. It continues to make an intellectual appeal in University circles, for it always seems to me (and I speak with respect to its leaders) to represent a state of attractive philosophic doubt; to expound its ideas in the general, but seldom to condescend to particulars. It certainly does not constitute an alternative government.

Now, though its intellectual qualities may be high, this can produce its own defects in practical politics.

It casts itself for the role of a third party, hoping, under some circumstances of close numbers in the House of Commons between Labour and Conservative, to represent the balance of power. But, and my experience confirms this conclusion, a party which aims at power in its own right, and therefore looks for the acceptance of national responsibility, must formulate and advocate its own policies of action with both broadness and particularity. It is not hoping simply to play off one great party against another.

When, therefore, we decided to call the new and united party the Liberal Party, we were adopting no analogy to the Liberal Party in the United Kingdom. On the contrary, we were aiming at political progress and power in our own right. We took the name 'Liberal' because we were determined to be a progressive party, willing to make experiments, in no sense reactionary but believing in the individual, his rights, and his enterprise, and rejecting the Socialist panacea.

In the United States of America, the word 'liberal' is used in contradistinction to 'conservative', but it seems, in recent years, to have acquired a special connotation. When I resided in America for some months in 1966-7, I thought that it threatened to become a word which had special reference to racial relations; to 'civil rights'; to the vexed questions of 'integration' and 'segregation'.

Thanks to a wise immigration policy, we are free of this problem in Australia, and I hope that we shall never permit ourselves to acquire it.

The next matter which required emphasis at the Canberra meeting was, 'what should be the substance of a Liberal policy?'

It was quite plain that 1944 was a crucial year for Australian politics. Labour had just had a smashing victory, and the Opposition, in the country though not in the House, was dejected and divided. Labour could afford to look to the future with great Socialist hopes. For the war, under both party administrations, had caused a tremendous growth in the powers of Government, in the all-pervading habit of receiving and obeying government orders. Private enterprise had grown accustomed to its chains. Private citizens had become familiar with the manifestations of the planned state; investment control, food rationing, petrol rationing, very high rates of taxation, government organisation of industry and transport.

If things were allowed to settle down into a continuance of this political pattern, Labour's future would be bright, and that of its opponents shadowy indeed.

It is a political fact, well known in all parliamentary democracies, that defeat, unless it is defeat by a very narrow margin, tends to disunite the defeated. If one defeat is followed by others, disunity becomes a certainty. In Australia, even the massive monolithic unity of the Labour Party, to which I had referred at the Canberra Conference, could not survive the successive defeats suffered by it after 1949. It suffered grave internal divisions; a large group split off from it and formed a new Democratic Labour Party. It had conflicts in its branches; open conflict about its leaders; in short, everything that a political opponent could desire.

In 1944, it was clear that my main task, as Leader of the Opposition, was to secure the organic and mental unity of fourteen fractions. This, of course, was far more than a problem of mechanics. A unity artificially attained will not last long if there is no genuine community of thought; of basic principles and applied ideas. It was therefore necessary for me, as the promoter, to prepare the foundations for a comprehensive statement of political objectives. As I said to the Canberra Conference in 1944:

> We have, partly by own our fault and partly by some extremely clever propaganda by the Labour Party, been put into the position of appearing to resist political and economic progress. In other words, on far too many questions we have found our role to be simply that of the man who says 'no'.

> Once this atmosphere is created, it is quite simple for us to be branded as reactionaries, and, indeed, if we are not careful the very unsoundness of so many of Labour's political proposals may accustom us so much to the role

of critic that we become unduly satisfied with our existing state of affairs.

There is no room in Australia for a party of reaction. There is no useful place for a policy of negation.

I then proceeded to set out what I believed should be our 'ultimate objectives'. It would be tedious to repeat them in detail; but in substance they amounted to a series of propositions relating to international and domestic, political and economic affairs.

Internationally, we should seek peace and security from external aggression by living 'in the closest communion with Commonwealth and other like countries'. That meant that we saw a wise foreign policy as part of our defence, though we also came out clearly for treating National defence, in the military field, as a matter of universal duty. At that time, of course, with the war going on, we were not in conflict with Labour on these points.

I therefore concentrated a good deal of attention on the domestic principles which the Australian people should be asked to adopt, so that, when peace came, Australia could move into an era in which there should be rapid development and growth, and a high degree of financial stability; two ideals thought by many to be irreconcilable. Now, how were we to secure development? Clearly, we were to encourage thrift and saving, investment, and reward.

The principle of such reward, sometimes sneered at as exhibiting the profit motive, is the dynamic force of social progress and is of the essence of what we call private or individual enterprise.

I will quote a few more passages from my speech on that historic occasion. I am not doing this in any spirit of vanity, or because I think that I was the sole Apostle (though I did have both the initiative and the chief responsibility). I record them because, as it happened, I wrote them in my own crabbed hand in my own office.

At the time, they were an individual effort. Later events were to show that I was by no means alone: I will come to them.

> We must aim at the growing exploitation of our natural resources. Governments do not provide enterprise; *they provide controls*. No sensible person can doubt that the revival of private enterprise is essential to post-war recovery and progress...

> There cannot be rising living standards if all we propose to do is redistribute what we now have. We must produce more and produce it more cheaply if we are to survive and grow.

I recognised, of course, that the State had its part to play, in major public works, in fiscal policy, in the provision of basic services, in the providing of national research and leadership. But it was not to be the Master.

> In a vision of the future, therefore, I see the individual and his encouragement and recognition as the prime motive force for the building of a better world. Socialism means high costs, inefficiency, the constant intrusion of political considerations, the damping down of enterprise, the overlordship of routine. None of these elements can produce progress, and without progress security will turn out to be a delusion.

These views did not represent a belief that private enterprise should have an 'open go'. Not at all. My friends and I recognized the economic responsibilities of the State to assist in preventing the recurrence of large-scale unemployment by appropriate economic and monetary measures; to secure, through social legislation, a decent and reasonable measure of economic security and material well-being for all responsible citizens; and to succeed in both of these purposes by creating a state of affairs which would encourage the enterprise, resourcefulness, and efficiency of individuals and to lead to the greatest possible output of the needed goods and services.

This seems commonplace now. It expresses views which were held by many in 1944; but it needed saying in a public and comprehensive way.

That Conference was a great success; a success to which many delegates made a valuable contribution. It would be self-defeating to name most or all of them. But I shall always remember two people who typified the prevailing spirit; Mrs Couchman (later Dame Elizabeth) and W.H. (later Sir William) Anderson.

'May' Couchman (as I knew her) had a clear mind and a practical grasp of politics. She had for a long time been President of the Australian Women's National League in Victoria. It was a fine body; its members did far more electoral work than most men; it had a history and tradition, and a natural pride in its own identity. It was not easy for it to merge itself into a new nation-wide organisation and become part of the Women's Section of the Liberal Party.

Yet within six months, Mrs Couchman, with the aid of loyal colleagues, had achieved it!

W.H. Anderson was, and is, a man of seemingly dry but

precise mind, a patriot with a lifetime of service in war and peace. He had been sufficiently dissatisfied with the Opposition to form and lead the Services and Citizens Party, one of the fourteen 'fractions' called to Canberra.

I had discussed the problem with him in my home at Kew, in Melbourne, and was greatly stimulated by his pungent remarks. He played a great hand at Canberra, and later at Albury. With no personal ambitions for Parliamentary office, he has remained a driving force in the Liberal Party organisation ever since. He was Federal President for some years. One could always get up an argument with him; but, to me, he typifies the whole spirit of the 'founding fathers' (and mothers) of the Great Australian Liberal Revival.

Well, as I have recounted, the Canberra Conference not only declared for unity, but decided on a name and on broadly-stated objectives.

It was agreed that the delegates would report back to their respective organisations and recommend that the decisions of the Conference be carried into effect. A further plenary Conference would then be held at Albury, in New South Wales, at which, it was anticipated, the new Party would be formally constituted, and a Constitution adopted.

So promptly did all the delegations act and report back that by 31 October I was able to send out from my legal Chambers in Melbourne a circular letter to each organisation represented at the Canberra Conference, indicating the nature of the responses I had received.

It gives me pleasure to recall them. The President of the Liberal Democratic Party in New South Wales, E.K. White, a most resolute character; Neville Harding, Chairman of the

Democratic Party of New South Wales (who became Lord Mayor of Sydney); W.H. Anderson and the General Secretary of the United Australia Organization in Victoria, and Mrs Couchman; the Queensland, South Australia, and Tasmanian organizations, had all come enthusiastically into line.

Fortified by these events, I sat down to do a mort of work, though I was now assisted by many carefully considered suggestions and drafts, on the preparation of a Constitution and a Platform. I am grateful to recall that, with much debate and proper amendments, my efforts were in general approved.

Three matters properly engaged much attention and inspired most lively contributions.

The first was the proposal that we should have a Federal organization, meaning by that one in which State Divisions should have complete autonomy on State political matters; Federal matters being the special concern of a Federal Executive, Council, and Secretariat. This, in a country very sensitive about 'State Rights', was not easy of achievement, but it was accepted.

The second concerned the ways and means of working out policy. There should be a Policy Committee in each State, and, for the Commonwealth, a Committee partly Parliamentary and partly representing the Branches or the Divisions. We provided for these Committees. But it took a few years, and a good deal of discussion, to establish what was to me basic; that is, that the Federal platform of the Party, its broad objectives, should be moulded, with recommendations by the Committees, by the Annual Federal Council, but that the particular Election policy must be propounded by the Federal Leader in consultation with his Parliamentary colleagues. It was very important to establish this principle, since one of our great criticisms of the Labour Party was that every Labour Member of Parliament, from the leader down, was bound to accept the directions of the non-Parliamentary Federal Executive of the Labour Party; the 'thirty-six faceless men', as we were later to describe them with devastating effect.

And so, the twin ideas of Organisation control of the Platform and Parliamentary Party control of Election policy within the broad principles of the Platform, were established.

The third problem concerned the ways and means of financing the new party. The old United Australia Party, except for a very nominal membership fee, had been financed by special and largely self-appointed bodies. Thus, in Sydney there was a Consultative Council made up of eminent businessmen, who 'raised the wind' and met the expenses of the State Organisation, and, in my experience, did not hesitate to say what policies should be pursued. In Melbourne, there was a similar body, the 'National Union', also composed of eminent citizens, which paid the expenses of the State organisation but did not, in my experience, give orders. But the position was most unsatisfactory. The Liberal Party was bound to be accused, by the Labour Party propagandists, of being the servants of 'Big Business'. It must be made evident that we were not; it must be made expressly clear that the new Party organization would raise and control its own finances. This was done.

By this time, we were about to enter 1946, a General Election Year. Our Joint Standing Committee met in Canberra in January 1946, and composed, for the first time, the 'Federal Platform of the Liberal Party of Australia'.

We stated our objectives.

In the light of subsequent developments, I should quote

a few of them. We declared that we wanted to have an Australian Nation

In which an intelligent, free, and liberal Australian democracy shall be maintained by

(a)   Parliament controlling the Executive and the Law controlling all;

(b)   Freedom of speech, religion, and association;

(c)   Freedom of citizens to choose their own way of life, subject to the rights of others;

(d)   Protecting the people against exploitation;

(e)   Looking primarily to the encouragement of individual initiative and enterprise as the dynamic force of reconstruction and progress.

As so much was to turn upon domestic economic policy in the succeeding years, I should go on to quote a few relevant passages of the Platform. Increased production was clearly going to be needed after the austerities of war. So we used such phrases as:

> Favouring the principles that wages should be the highest and conditions the best that the industry concerned can provide, and that good work is the essential condition of good pay, we shall conduct a constant educational campaign against the doctrine that the interests of employer and employee are opposed...

> ...Increased, more efficient and cheaper production are the essential conditions of new and increased markets, regular employment, and rising standards of living for those engaged in industry...

> ...Increasing production demands increasing markets. Increasing markets can be won if production of

> commodities is both good and cheap. Cheap production depends upon effort and efficiency, not upon wage-slashing. We believe that high wages and high production are natural and inevitable allies.

In that same year, the Labour Government introduced and carried a Law for the broadcasting of Parliamentary proceedings. I make some personal reference to this in a subsequent chapter. But politically, it proved to be a Government mistake. Those citizens who 'listened in' – and, except on a few extraordinary occasions, they were a small minority – were fascinated by the attack, and somewhat uninterested in the defence. So, on the air, we, the Opposition, made headway.

Numerically, we were a small Opposition, though we developed a considerable *esprit de corps*, organized our debates, and heartily enjoyed them.

The General Election of 1946 fell in October. Our organization was relatively new; there were still some teething troubles. It was not reasonable to expect to win the many seats that would be needed to put the Government out. We won a few seats, and were unlucky not to win a few more. As I wrote to Arthur Fadden shortly afterwards: 'When you consider that the task was to arrest the momentum of Labour, and then to secure some movement in the opposite direction, the result of the election is not unsatisfactory.'

I might have added, in the old French aphorism, that 'it is the first step that counts'.

But although those of us who were the toilers in the vineyard were not depressed, we had plenty of onlookers who, having contributed little or nothing to victory, at once became critical. Before long, the word went around that 'You can't win with Menzies!' It received no acceptance from my Parliamentary colleagues; but in a few newspaper circles it had powerful support.

One newspaper of large circulation published, having, I suspected, promoted it, a Public Opinion Poll which found that most people would like to replace me. This newspaper sent a reporter (a man whom I knew and liked) to get my comments. 'We have a story that at your Party meeting your leadership is coming under review and possibly challenged.'

As this story was completely false, I spoke my mind, and went so far as to say that it was quite characteristic of his employers, who were by nature destructive.

He reported this back, as I knew and intended that he should. A day or two later, I received a withering blast by letter, a letter in which I was accused of promoting my own 'supposed interests', to which I replied. It is an old controversy, and I have no desire to mention names now that I am out of the arena. But I did say two things which are worth recording for the benefit of my successors in politics, and, in particular, of my family.

My correspondent had, as I have said, made a slighting reference to my 'supposed interests'. My reply on that point was:

> Why *my* supposed interests? Can you really believe that you can strike down the leader of a Party (when you do not suggest any alternative leader in the Parliamentary ranks) and do no injury to the Party? Do you really believe that I have preferred my own interests?
>
> If the Prime Ministership is the crown of political ambition, I have worn it. After many years of thankless public work, in which my character and reputation have been assailed publicly and privately, I might with reason have returned to a profession in which, had I remained at it, I should have been relatively well-off and immune from

malice and abuse. But instead of returning to a private life, I undertook the leadership of a defeated Opposition, the creation of a new Liberal Party and the formulation of a policy which has received high praise from your own newspaper. With all respect, I dispute your right to make slighting references to my 'supposed interests' under the circumstances... The truth is that you have a notion that it is the privilege of the press to give criticism and the function of the politician to receive it meekly and with gratitude. When you have had to suffer one tiny fraction of the criticism and personal attack to which I have been subjected for years, you will perhaps be less ready to resent a gesture of annoyance and a little more appreciative of public service which, however human and frequently mistaken, has at any rate been honest and sustained.

Meanwhile, political history in Australia was being made. As I have tried to make clear, it was our firmly-held belief that the great issue to which Liberalism must direct itself was that of Socialism. It must be taken out of the academic realms of the debating society, and presented as a real issue of practical politics.

This would not be easy, for, as I have said, people had become accustomed to government control. But our opponents, not for the first or last time, raised the issue for us, and made it a living thing.

The incoming Chifley Government, in 1945, had decided to nationalize the Civil Air Services, which had in fact been pioneered by private enterprise with notable success. I remind my readers that the Labour scheme was, first to create a National Airlines Commission with power to conduct air services on behalf of the Government, and then, by a series of Statutory devices, give it a monopoly, thus eliminating the private services. On challenge, the High Court had found that the creation of a monopoly in inter-state air services violated Section 92 of the Australian Constitution, which guarantees the freedom of inter-state trade, commerce, and intercourse.

But the Socialist Objective, in which Chifley firmly believed, had been given a practical significance in the public mind. By 1948, the next great example had emerged. The Government passed laws to nationalize banking, under the circumstances and with the results I have earlier described.

The issue of Socialism was no longer academic. It came alive, and the critics subsided.

The 1949 General Election in Australia needs some special mention in any book of mine. The Labour Government had, in relation to both aviation and banking, prepared the ground for the kind of political battle which my colleagues and I had sought. We decided, with the complete concurrence of the Country Party, our close and almost indistinguishable ally, to fight the battle on the obvious ground. In the Policy Speech, which I wrote after consultation with my colleagues in the Opposition Executive, I stated the case as clearly, indeed as starkly, as I could; for I knew that we were at the crossroads.

I will quote just a few paragraphs:

> This is our great year of decision. Are we for the Socialist State, with its subordination of the individual to the universal officialdom of government, or are we for the ancient British faith that governments are the servants of the people?...

> ...The case against Socialism is a deadly one. It concerns the spiritual, mental, and physical future of our families...

> ...The best people in this community are not those who 'leave it to the other fellow', but those who by thrift and

self-sacrifice establish homes and bring up families and add to the national pool of savings and hope some day to sit 'under their own vine and fig-tree', owing nothing to anybody...

And then, to go to the heart of Liberalism, I said:

...The real freedoms are to worship, to think, to speak, to choose, to be ambitious, to be independent, to be industrious, to acquire skill, to seek reward. These are the real freedoms, for these are of the essence of the nature of man.

I have never regretted or qualified these words. The electors agreed with them.

And so, in December 1949, we achieved office and responsibility. We have retained it, with popular approval, ever since. In our first years, in the early fifties, we were to find ourselves coping with very great financial instability, with waves of inflation and an unhealthy loan market. But a steadfast adherence to our beliefs carried us through troubled waters; so successfully that for many years now Australia has (in spite of sceptics) enjoyed a period of unexampled growth with great financial stability and high credit, both domestically and internationally. 'Luck,' our opponents used to say. But I always remember the frequently forgotten words of the Book of Common Prayer – 'Good luck have thou with thine honour!' A little luck is no bad thing to have; I have had some experience of its opposite; but ideas and determination are of essence.

To such of my readers as have attended to this narrative, I would wish to add one observation. If my story seems to dwell on my own actions and words in this period of Liberal Revival, the simple reason is that, in the events that had happened, the duty and initiative fell upon me. I had to do that duty and maintain that initiative. With great help, as I proudly acknowledge; but the task imposed burdens which were, in a real sense, mine. If, in my retirement, I permit myself to cast myself for the role of the 'founding father' of a great and enduring Australian party, I hope that this will be attributed, not to a species of vanity, but to a just pride in a result which many 'practical' people would have dismissed from their imaginations twenty-three years ago.

www.ingramcontent.com/pod-product-compliance
Lightning Source LLC
Chambersburg PA
CBHW050539270326
41926CB00015B/3299